Let Them Play

Let Them Play

AN EARLY LEARNING (UN)CURRICULUM

Jeff A. Johnson
and Denita Dinger

Redleaf Press®
www.redleafpress.org
800-423-8309

Published by Redleaf Press
10 Yorkton Court
St. Paul, MN 55117
www.redleafpress.org

First edition 2012
Cover design by Jim Handrigan
Cover photograph courtesy of Heather Jones
Interior design by Jim Handrigan
Photographs on pages 30, 65, 178, and 194 by Jeff A. Johnson
Photographs on pages 6, 9, 11, 33, 46, 53, 74, 76, 88, 142, 161, 167, 169, 170, 181, 183, 189, 190, 191, 193, 209, and 212 by Denita Dinger
Photographs on pages xvi, 7, 18, and 197 by Brandi Seals
Photographs on pages 13, 50, 67, 103, 152, and 197 by Lynn A. Manfredi/Petitt
Photographs on pages by 24, 28, 98, 133, 176, 195, 197, 199, and 200 by Lisa Ditlefsen
Photographs on pages 36, 42, 47, and 197 by Jennifer Brosnahan
Photographs on pages 80 and 112 by Shelley Gagnon
Photograph on page 63 (top) by Amanda Jones
Photograph on page 63 (bottom) by Trisha David (www.trishadavidphotography.com)
Photograph on page 82 by Heather Jones
Typeset in Adobe Caslon Pro and Myriad Pro
Printed in the United States of America
19 18 17 16 15 14 13 12   1 2 3 4 5 6 7 8

Library of Congress Cataloging-in-Publication Data
Johnson, Jeff A., 1969-
    Let them play : an early learning (un)curriculum / Jeff A. Johnson and Denita Dinger.
    p. cm.
    Summary: "Playtime is focused, purposeful, and full of learning. This (un)curriculum is all about fostering children's play, trusting children as capable and engaged learners, and leaving behind boxed curriculums and prescribed activities"— Provided by publisher.
    Includes bibliographical references.
    ISBN 978-1-60554-053-5 (pbk.)
    1. Play—United States. 2. Early childhood education—United States. 3. Early childhood education—Curricula—United States.   I. Dinger, Denita. II. Title.
    LB1139.35.P55J65 2012
    372.210973—dc23
                        2011041149

Printed on acid-free paper

To my children, Myah and Landon, as well as my day care kids. They have been the best teachers I could ever ask for, reminding me daily to slow down, enjoy, and appreciate the learning in unplanned moments.

—*Denita*

To my mom, Lynn Johnson, for buying me those wooden blocks and then letting me play.

—*Jeff*

Contents

Foreword by Lisa Murphy, Ooey Gooey, Inc. ix

Preface xiii

Acknowledgments xv

Chapter 1: What Happened to "Go Play"? 1
    Play-Focused Learning 5
    What Happened to "Go Play"? 11
    Why the Rush? 16
    Is Rushing Worthwhile? 20
    Where Are We Rushing To? 22

Chapter 2: Defining an (Un)Curriculum 25
    What an (Un)Curriculum Is Not 27
    Characteristics of an (Un)Curriculum 28
    Push the Curriculum Back Up 48

Chapter 3: Supporting an (Un)Curriculum 51
    Trust Your Employees. 52
    Focus on Art 56
    Truly Value Play 59
    Encourage Activist Caregivers 60
    Overcome Fear 62
    Seek Out Simplicity 65
    Value Vacation Mind-Sets 68

Chapter 4: Creating Engaging Spaces 77
    Happy BRAINS 80
    Engaged SENSES 81
    Safe DANGER 84
    Abundant TIME 87

Unbridled CHITCHAT 89
Predictable CHANGE 90
Thoughtful STIMULATION 91
Appropriate CHALLENGE. 94
Real WORK 95
Perpetual MOTION 96

Chapter 5:   Trusting Kids to Learn 99
             Emotional Environments 100
             Trusting Children. 113

Chapter 6:   (Un)Planning 143
             Throw Away Your Lesson Plan Book. 149
             Be an Early Learning Experience Architect. 153
             Practice the Principles of (Un)Planning 154

Chapter 7:   Taking Baby Steps 179
             Denita's Story 180
             Experiment and Shake Things Up 192

Chapter 8:   Tests, Evaluations, and Assessments . . . Oh My! 201
             Don't Feed the Beast. 205
             Assess and Evaluate This 207
             Trust Children's Self-Assessment and Self-Evaluation. 207
             Document. 210
             Do Something with Documentation 213

References   217

Suggested Reading 219

Suggested Websites and Blogs 223

Foreword

I heard about Jeff Johnson long before I met him, when an enthusiastic conference attendee told me, "He's like a male Bev Bos!" She went on to say that Jeff was the coauthor of *Do-It-Yourself Early Learning*, a book filled with great ideas for things you could make yourself with just a couple visits to your local home improvement store—to which I replied, "OMG! I just ordered that book!" I'd ordered it because I was intrigued by the slightly punk–DIY connection, and I thought it would be cool to have some of that *l'esprit du punk* in an early childhood environment. And though I loved the book, my respect for Jeff deepened not when he taught me how to make a swamp in my sensory tub or launch ping-pong balls using a homemade catapult, but when I read these words of his: "Children are curious, not suicidal." I knew immediately that anyone who had the chutzpah to put pen to paper to write and publish such a bold (and true!) statement was destined to become a friend and colleague of mine. And I'm proud to say he has.

When Jeff asked me to write the foreword for his new book, which he coauthored with Denita Dinger, I was honored and amazed—and then the fear and intimidation moved in. Just what had I committed to? What would I say? This was their rodeo, after all. How do you even write a foreword? Give me guidelines! Give me instructions! (And this I requested of a dude who keeps dead squirrels in jars and brings them to dinner if you ask him nicely.) Jeff said he trusted me to write what I needed to say. So I thank him for his trust and the opportunity, and I am grateful for his supportive team at Redleaf Press, who said they'd help me clean up my writing style, chock-full of run-on sentences and lacking appropriate punctuation.

In *Let Them Play,* which I affectionately refer to as the (un)curriculum book, Jeff and Denita encourage providers in both center and family child care programs to stretch their willingness to engage in honest self-reflection and really examine what they call "curriculum." They invite you to go deeper than simply claiming to be play based. They invite you to become play *obsessed.*

Now it's no secret that Jeff probably asked me to do this foreword because he knows that I'm already play obsessed to the core. In fact, I joked to my husband after reading the manuscript, "Well, shoot! Jeff and Denita have just saved me a helluvalotta of time! Because of this [waves manuscript in air], I won't need to write my next book!" And while there are many resources out there that can help early childhood educators take the leap from traditional to emergent curriculum, what I really appreciate about this book is that Jeff and Denita honor the fact that we all have various starting spots, that we're all at various points in our journey toward being more play obsessed. Jeff and Denita value baby steps and understand that becoming play obsessed is definitely a process.

The industry of early childhood education is filled with T-shirt slogans and bumper-sticker dogma: "Set the stage and facilitate!" "Be a guide on the side, not a sage on the stage!" We can all wear a "My program is play obsessed!" T-shirt, but only those of us who are willing to go deep and examine what we call "our program" will reap the true benefits of the investigative, introspective, hard work we do. *Let Them Play* will guide you on your investigative journey and show you how to push beyond the T-shirt slogan. The authors name-drop at the right moments to reinforce their position statements, and they provide a plethora of suggested readings that will keep many of us busy through to next year. But it's the manageable chunks of information that ultimately make *Let Them Play* a valuable resource for me. Examples include

- The four results of fear and hypersurveillance (page 64)

- The five elements of a truly child-centered program (pages 41–42)

- Three advocacy tips (pages 48–49)

- The seven programming guidelines that make an (un)curriculum possible (page 52)

- Five reasons society has lost faith in saying, "Go play" (pages 12–15)

- Eight reasons to throw away your lesson-planning books (pages 150–151)

- Nine problems with boxed, preplanned curriculums (page 16)

- The twelve principles of brain-based learning (page 31)

- The six characteristics of an (un)curriculum (page 29)

- The ten principles of physical spaces that permit children to be the boss of their own learning (page 79)

Depending on where you were trained, where you went to school, who mentored you, and what bandwagon the USA was riding when you cut your early childhood teeth, Jeff and Denita's message might be affirming or frightening. When I first started teaching and working in child care centers, I was told, "*This* is the theme. Now go plan activities that fit it." There's nothing wrong with predetermined themes, but there's a lot wrong with how they're often implemented: talking about XYZ topic Monday through Friday come hell or high water even if it has no context or relevancy to the children in the room. As I grew and was exposed to emergent curriculum, I started planning for the bones of the day but moved away from the themes. I started paying attention, observing, and using what I was seeing the children do as fodder and inspiration for deeper investigation. I played with language, and "theme" morphed into "projects"; "lesson planning" turned into "documentation and observations."

It can take time to change minds. We must be patient with ourselves, our programs, and our children. We must trust the process.

We must trust the children. We must trust our ability to create an appropriate and engaging environment. And finally, we must trust ourselves. Then and only then will we start moving to the sidelines of children's lives, which, as Anna Quindlen says, is "where we belong if we do our jobs right."

Lisa Murphy
Early Childhood Specialist
CEO and Founder
of Ooey Gooey, Inc.

Use your smartphone to scan this QR code to visit Lisa's website, or go to www.ooeygooey.com.

Lisa Murphy, BS, CEO and Founder of Ooey Gooey, Inc., has been involved in many aspects of early childhood education for over twenty years. She is the author of four books and conducts hundreds of training seminars each year. Like Denita and Jeff, Lisa encourages you to become play obsessed!

Preface

Over the last couple of decades, the world has changed and the early years have become too important and serious for mere child's play. We live in a world of prenatal curriculums and high-pressure preschools; a world where there's no longer time for dramatic play or recess; a world where childhood is rushed through and play is replaced by flash cards and worksheets. A January 2012 American Academy of Pediatrics article, published online, concludes its abstract by saying, "Societal priorities for young children—safety and school readiness—may be hindering children's physical development" (Copeland et al. 2012, 1). We believe they go farther than that. We believe these "societal priorities" are also hindering emotional, cognitive, and social development. The push for safety and academic learning, while well intentioned, has had unintended consequences. It has resulted in sterile, boring, and passionless early childhood programs that fail to trust children as learners. In the article, the authors say they were surprised to find that a "societal focus on 'academics' extended even to the preschool-aged group" they studied (Copeland et al. 2012, 6).

We were not surprised.

Anyone who has worked with children over the last few decades can share stories about the push toward formal academics—and away from play—in early learning programs. The loss of play is detrimental for all children, especially those living in poverty. Another American Academy of Pediatrics article, originally published online in December 2011, states, "For children who are underresourced to reach their highest potential, it is essential that parents, educators, and pediatricians recognize the importance of lifelong benefits that children gain from play" (Milteer and Ginsburg 2011, e204). That article concludes by saying,

"School systems are focused on overcoming their academic deficiencies in a safe environment often at the expense of time for arts, recess, physical education classes, and after-school activities that include playing, despite evidence that supports that what happens in play contributes substantially to social and emotional learning, even in the classroom" (Milteer and Ginsburg 2011, e210).

The slow but steady shift from play to academics may seem harmless in its increments, but it has negatively affected children's curiosity, creativity, social skills, self-regulation, problem-solving skills, knowledge of the world, and so much more. And let's not forget about fun. The rush through childhood and the push toward academics are sucking the fun out of childhood quicker than a five-year-old can suck the filling out of a Twinkie.

We don't like this world.

Let Them Play is our way of countering these changes and putting more filling into the Twinkie. We wrote *Let Them Play* to show caregivers of young children another way, a way that embraces play, trusts children as learners, and values childhood. We call this alternative to the current academic push an *(un)curriculum,* because it is built on a solid foundation of research and real-world experience, and it is also the antithesis of what currently happens in many early learning programs. In preparing to write the book, we read a lot and talked to hundreds of parents and caregivers in both center- and family-based programs. We also called on our own experiences as parents and professional caregivers. Between the two of us, we have over thirty years of down-on-the-floor-with-the-kids experience, the result of which is this book, based on scientific research and full of real-life examples of how to support child-led and play-based learning.

Our biggest hope is that the ideas and stories we share in *Let Them Play* will help you kindle a renewed passion for early learning, value play, and push back against the changes that are eroding away the best of childhood.

Use your smartphone to scan this QR code to visit our Let Them Play Facebook page, or go to www.facebook.com/LetThemPlayBook, where we continue the conversation about the importance of play.

Acknowledgments

We would both like to acknowledge Linda Hein and the great people at Redleaf Press who made this book possible: David Heath, Kyra Ostendorf, Laurie Herrmann, JoAnne Voltz, Inga Weberg, Paul Bloomer, Douglas Schmitz, Jim Handrigan, Carla Valadez, Heidi Hogg, Devin Kormanik, Renee Hammes, Eric Johnson, Shaun Ward, Cindy Haider, and Steven Rhoden. Oh, and Janet Ward. If you're reading this book, then it's because Janet made sure it was safely shipped.

Thanks to Beth Wallace for your fresh eyes and mindful editing. You're awesome.

Thanks to all the early learning professionals who shared stories, opinions, photos, and ideas. We don't have room to name you all here, but your experience, thoughtfulness, and dedication to children have been inspiring.

All of these people are Artists, not Cogs.

I would like to thank my husband for his unfailing support while I chase my dreams. I would also like to acknowledge "my Jenn" for all the times she's let me bounce ideas off of her, vent, cry, and laugh. She's been the best gift any family child care provider could ask for. Finally, I give a huge thank-you to Jeff for offering me the opportunity of a lifetime.

—Denita

Use your smartphone to scan this QR code to visit Denita's website, or go to www.playcounts.com.

A special thanks to my wife, Tasha, for putting up with all those random moments when my eyes darted up and off to the side as I contemplated, wrestled with, and composed this book in my head. Thanks to Denita for being just as bullheaded and opinionated as I am. Thanks to the Big Island and Starbucks 9602. I also need to thank my early learning buddy, Sue Erpelding of Providers Empowering Providers in Wyoming, for letting me delay projects I was working on for her to make time for this book.

—Jeff

Use your smartphone to scan this QR code to visit Jeff's website, or go to www .explorationsearlylearning .com.

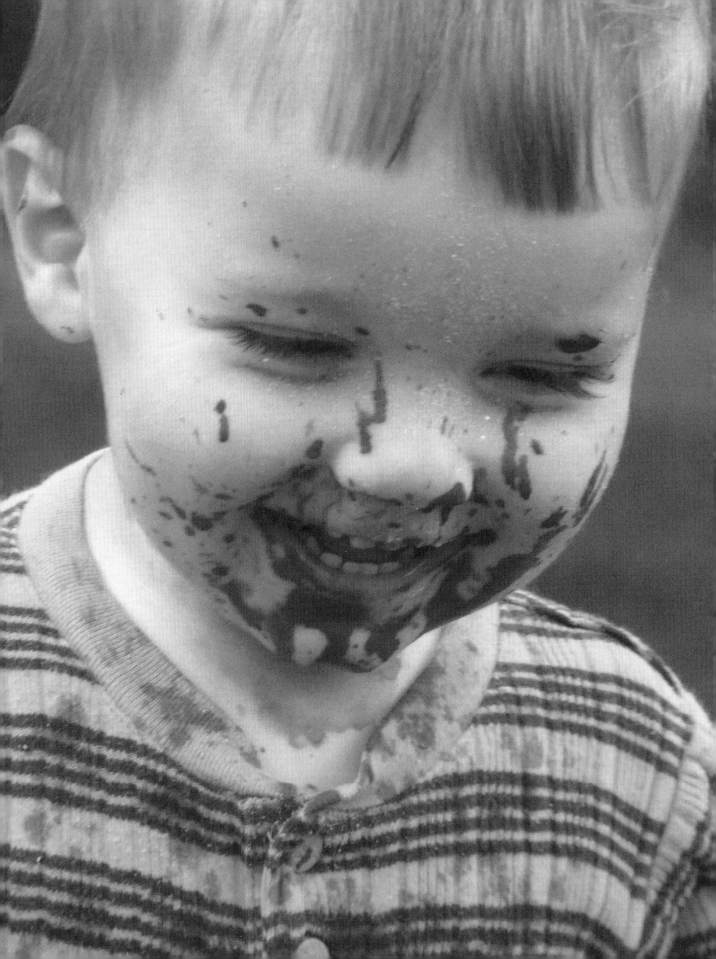

What Happened to "Go Play"?

Neuroscientists, developmental biologists, psychologists, social scientists, and researchers from every point of the scientific compass now know that play is a profound biological process. It has evolved over eons in many animal species to promote survival. It shapes the brain and makes animals smarter and more adaptable. In higher animals, it fosters empathy and makes possible complex social groups. For us, play lies at the core of creativity and innovation.

—Stuart Brown with Christopher Vaughan, *Play: How It Shapes the Brain, Opens the Imagination, and Invigorates the Soul*

"Jeff, can I eat snack later? School was tough today, and I need to play for a while before I eat."

—Jack, age five, after his third day of kindergarten

Play is not frivolous. It is not a luxury. It is not something to fit in after completing all the important stuff. Play *is* the important stuff. Play is a drive, a need, a brain-building must-do. It hardwires us as much as it centers us. It feeds our intellect as much as our imagination. It builds knowledge as much as empathy. It connects neurons, and it connects ideas. We could not be fully human without it. Yet good-intentioned people with legitimate social concerns are rushing children through

1

their childhoods, pushing developmentally inappropriate practices, and preventing children from their most important task: playing.

Let's look at what happened to Gabby:

Gabby sits in the middle of an old oak floor feeding a naked baby doll with a wooden block. Her legs crossed in front of her, she sways gently. A scabbed left knee—an apple tree climbing injury—pokes from under her brown and pink dress. Her bare toes wiggle the tune she is humming. After burping her baby with gentle back pats, she kisses its forehead and tucks it into a tattered shoe box for a nap. Gabby then tippy-toes silently to the other side of the room, where she helps another child prepare an imaginary magic princess banquet, talking in hushed tones while stirring bowls of make-believe cookie batter and grilling pretend steak. After the party, Gabby builds a house of wooden blocks and scraps of cardboard for a family of plastic cows; she reads a few favorite books to herself (she has had them memorized for months); she counts tiny plastic bugs ("one, two, three, seven, nine, eleven"); she argues loudly with a friend over who had a stuffed duck first; she eats lunch without spilling her milk much; she sleeps; she climbs the apple tree again, this time without falling.

Three-year-old Gabby spends her days busy at play. She is in charge of her curriculum, fluttering from activity to activity as her interests change. Gabby's caregiver maintains a strong emotional environment, provides a rich and varied physical environment, supports the interests of the children in her care, and gives them as much autonomy as they can manage. She does her best to step back and let the children guide their own learning. To the untrained eye, Gabby's play looks chaotic, but her hands-on engagement with the environment is focused, purposeful, and full of learning. She is mastering her body, learning language, honing social skills, thinking creatively, and making cognitive leaps as she stacks blocks and rocks dolls. She is a learning machine out to understand the world and her place in it.

Gabby's mother, however, feels a lot of pressure from her friends (who are also mothers of young children) to enroll Gabby in an academic preschool program to make sure she'll be ready to start learning in kindergarten. And while Jenny thinks her daughter is a bright bulb, she doesn't have a lot of proof; after all, Gabby spends all her time "just playing" in her current provider's program, and the academic preschool advertises "an academic curriculum designed to prepare students for school," which placates Jenny's fears. The academic program promises regular evaluations and even tests Gabby before enrolling her.

Gabby begins attending the new program three days a week for three hours each day. Her time there is broken up into chunks of no more than thirty minutes, which means numerous transitions and no time for self-directed free play. Initially Gabby is in a classroom with other three-year-olds, but in less than a month, she turns four and is moved to another room with another set of kids and teachers. Self-confident, curious, apple tree–climbing Gabby keeps to herself. Every once in a while, she tosses a fit for her mother and begs to "go back to Miss Cindy's house." Jenny writes these changes off as part of growing up.

In a syrupy, singsong voice, one of the four part-time caregivers staffing Gabby's new preschool classroom explains to ten fidgety children exactly where on the construction paper frogs they should glue the googly eyes so the frogs will be pretty. "If it's pretty," she says, "then your mommy will like it and hang it up." Gabby seems lost. She's not used to being still for so long. She's not used to this sort of boxed curriculum, to precut project pieces, and to having so little control over her time and energy. She makes a sea of glue on the frog's chest, dips the googly eyes into the glue, and places one on the frog's front left foot and the other on the center of its face. Then she jumps out of her chair and frog-hops across the room to the baby dolls. She is scolded and placed in time-out, where—still in frog mode—she tries to catch a passing fly with her tongue. When she gets up, it's free time, but not the kind of "free" she's used to. She and a redheaded boy who was also in time-out are assigned to the block area. They have to put in fifteen minutes of free time there before they can move to the dramatic play area, and then, after another fifteen minutes, they get to use the playdough. They try to sneak a couple of big yellow trucks into the block area from the car area but are told that today the trucks aren't allowed with the blocks. Gabby and the redheaded boy are scolded for not listening, and then they start building a block tower. It's a sturdy tower on a strong foundation, and soon they need to drag a chair over to keep building—and then they find themselves back in time-out for making such a tall, "dangerous" structure.

What passes as child's play in many early learning programs today is planned, regulated, organized, supervised, and documented by adults to the point that the lightheartedness, spontaneity, and freedom that define childhood no longer exist. Gabby went from hours of autonomous play every day to an environment that was so overly controlled and regimented that her free time was planned out for her. Her curiosity and creativity went from being nurtured to being punished. The pilfering of Gabby's play-based learning was not malicious: everyone in her life wanted the best for her. Still, the unrelenting and misguided push for early academics and school achievement took away the autonomy and joy from Gabby's learning. The new environment transformed her from a child eager for self-discovery and new experiences into an unsure and timid little girl. Gabby learned that she could avoid time-out and scoldings by gluing the frog eyes where the teacher said to glue them, by *not* taking initiative, and by *not* being creative. After a few months in the new program, Gabby seemed . . . diminished.

On her first day of kindergarten, Gabby is excited and nervous. She has a bright new pair of Mary Janes and a scuff-free backpack, and her long hair spills like a fountain from the top of her head. She has reason to be nervous: the school district expects Gabby to know today what her mom knew at the end of kindergarten, because the curriculum has been accelerated. There will be more worksheets and tests for Gabby; not as much art, music, gym, and recess as her mom had; and little time for play. The magical playhouse that anchored the kindergarten classroom for a generation has been removed to make way for three computers. The dress-up clothes, kitchen supplies, dolls, and building blocks went with it. The kindergarten teacher says she knows the school is pushing kids too hard. "I feel it in my bones," she says. Gabby's teacher would like her students to have more time to play, but she is under local, state, and federal pressure to make sure the kids in her class achieve certain learning benchmarks— whether they are developmentally ready or not.

Gabby feels the pressure, too, and she senses her teacher's stress. Some days her tummy hurts and she begs to stay home. Her lips are red and badly chapped from nervous licking—a condition that magically clears up during school breaks.

What if Gabby's mom hadn't felt so worried and pressured to move Gabby to an academic program? What if Gabby had stayed with Miss Cindy and had been allowed to "just play" until it was time for her to start kindergarten? What if her kindergarten teacher had been able to allow the children in her class to learn through play, as so many earlier generations of kindergartners had? What if parents, caregivers, and early educators shifted their mind-sets and *really* trusted play as a teacher and *really* trusted children as capable learners?

Childhood has changed. Listen to one parent and teacher we questioned for this book, who grew up in the 1950s:

> One of my most vivid memories [of childhood] is playing "Wagon Train" with neighborhood children. Backyard Adirondack chairs were our wagons. We wore discarded adult garments as our dress-up clothes and picked berries and leaves to make mud pies. We stayed outdoors for hours, going in only to eat lunch or use the bathroom. We got along, and if there was a problem, we settled our own disputes without fights. We used our imaginations and were very creative.

Mary and her playmates were given freedom to play on their own for hours at a time. They decided how to spend their time and engage the world. Along the way, they built strong bodies, learned to solve problems, developed social skills, flexed their imaginations, grew their intellects, and had a ton of fun. Encouraging such play-focused learning is a core goal of this book.

Play-Focused Learning

Play is an inborn learning strategy. When asked why play is important, Peter Gray, research professor of psychology at Boston College and author of the *Freedom to Learn* blog at www.psychologytoday.com, responded, "Can you imagine life without play? How dreary it would be.

Life, liberty, and the pursuit of happiness. The pursuit of happiness is play. Moreover, play is how we learn, how we make friends, how we find meaning in life."

Many people know that play is not what it used to be. We surveyed over a hundred parents, professional caregivers, and child advocates from three continents, seeking their stories, thoughts, and feelings about play and early learning. When we asked them to compare childhood today with their own childhoods, some common ideas emerged:

- **Children have less autonomy.**

    "Children's lives today are much more scheduled."

    "Children are so limited in what they can do and think."

    "I had much, much more freedom."

    "The type of freedom I had as a child doesn't exist for children today."

- **Play has changed.**

    "I often wonder if our kids are missing out on some of the opportunities to be creative and explore on their own because of our schedules and structured activities."

"When I was a kid, there was real play."

"Imaginative play is not fostered."

"[There is] less outside play and pretend play for the majority of children."

"Play was respected just as much as schoolwork."

"There's not a lot of creative, imaginative play. When I was growing up, we didn't have all of the realistic toys. We had to improvise."

"We had some toys, sure, like Barbie—but they were more open-ended then. Now everything is press a button and make a noise. And the marketers are telling parents that pressing a button will make their kids smarter. It's a lie."

"Children today don't play with mud pies or dig up worms or make kites from junk."

"I think kids today are too regimented, running from activity to activity with no time to just be."

- **Adults are more fearful.**

  "With today's safety issues, it's not possible to send kids outside and tell them to be home for lunch. But some of my fondest memories are of going exploring and playing by the creek."

  "Children are not left alone, [so] they are not making and learning from their own mistakes because [an adult is] right there to fix it."

  "I don't think it is any more dangerous, but there is always doubt and someone to blame if something happens."

  "I panic if my daughter's school bus is late."

  "I think society is so fearful today that children miss the simple things, such as climbing trees, and are not allowed to be independent. The rules and regulations abounding in child care don't allow for exploration and learning from mistakes."

  "Today you are too scared to let your kids go out on their own."

- **Children grow up faster.**

  "[Children] start sports, dance, and school so much earlier, they aren't allowed to be children."

  "Our kids are being asked to grow up too fast. I keep telling mine to be kids as long as they can. If that means dressing up or playing with dolls, do it—do what you feel desire to do. It's not right that ten-year-olds have to worry about 'being cool' so they can't play with dolls anymore, and dress-up is only cool if you're dressing up like Hannah Montana."

  "I think girls' inappropriate clothing and makeup is starting at an earlier age. I remember my first thing of makeup was clear mascara in seventh grade!"

  "Today's children are under a lot more pressure to perform, either at school or in sports, ballet, etc."

- **Modern kids are more sedentary; electronics have replaced outside play.**

  "Outside play until the streetlights came on was common."

"I definitely had more opportunities to play outside with little or no supervision."

"Children don't play outdoors as much. They seem to prefer television and video games."

"Outdoor and imaginative play seemed to be more abundant."

"We get kids hooked on TV and computers from birth, but we're not outside playing and having picnics and exploring the world."

But perhaps it's just a case of fond memories clouding clear thinking. We humans tend to have overly fond memories of our own childhoods; we gloss over the bad bits and glorify the good. Viewing the past through rose-tinted glasses is nothing new. Back in 10,000 BCE, little Ogg Jr. sat by the campfire playing with a stack of smooth, glossy rocks while his parents, Bunny and Ogg Oggerson Sr., reminisced about how much better the dingy, pointy rocks of their childhoods were. It's human nature to think everything was better back in the day.

On the other hand, many of the people we surveyed shared the dark parts of their early years too. We heard stories of abuse, poverty, divorce, and other trauma. While nobody had a perfect childhood, it is clear that some things have changed. One big difference is that Bunny and Ogg, Mary, and the others quoted above survived their early childhoods without a formal curriculum defining the course for their learning. These folks were born wired for play, they played unmonitored and free, and they learned. For most of them, adult involvement in their early learning ended with two words: "Go play." The curriculum for their early years was an *(un)curriculum*. For most of human history, adults have been too busy avoiding saber-toothed tigers, procuring food and shelter, and creating and destroying civilizations to pay much attention to the day-to-day minutiae of their children's lives. In his book *Childhood in World History*, Peter N. Stearns explains that for most of world history, children have been free to be children during their youngest years. They were often required to contribute to the welfare of the group at an early age, but "childhood was undoubtedly a time of play."

Need more proof that society is hurrying childhood along? As we write, the Obama administration has states scrambling to secure a piece of the $4.35 billion Race to the Top Fund. Let's look at that name— Race to the Top. It implies a sense of urgency and a need to rush forward. While the race is to get "to the top," it also implies that those who do not work hard enough will be losers left at the bottom. In the end, it draws on the same well-intentioned desire for success and fear of being unprepared for the unknowable future that are rushing childhood along. The US Department of Education (2009) website says, "Awards in Race to the Top will go to states that are leading the way with ambitious yet achievable plans for implementing coherent, compelling, and comprehensive education reform"—whatever that means. We assume that a committee of government lawyers under the influence of freeway exhaust fumes or hard liquor composed the prose on this website. We were unable to decipher the slippery and obtuse language enough to understand exactly *why* there is a race and precisely *what* everyone is racing to the top of.

This fund could bring positive change in our schools, and we hope it does. Only time will tell. We know that the name is scary and that the government's track record is not great when it comes to improving education. The quality of education in our public schools has not changed much over the last few decades, but spending has shot up like the blood pressure of a senator confronted by angry citizens at a town hall meeting.

While per pupil funding has more than doubled since the 1970s, similar gains in student achievement have not followed with increasing federal funding for education (Lips, Watkins, and Fleming 2008). Past efforts at education reform have not met with much success. No Child Left Behind has pushed the elementary curriculum into preschools to the point that three-year-olds are expected to behave and achieve like five-year-olds, and Head Start has morphed from focusing on social competence to emphasizing academics. This time around things could be different, but we aren't going to hold our breath.

What Happened to "Go Play"?

It appears that (mostly) well-meaning experts have convinced us that the child-created (un)curriculums that served humankind so well for so long are something to be feared. Too many parents have been convinced by experts that letting Bobby and Briana make mud pies, splash in puddles, stack blocks, and baby baby dolls will not prepare them for school, or work, or marriage, or life, or whatever it is children are being prepared for. Society is afraid that little Bobby and Briana will end up slack jawed and stupid if it fails to map out learning objectives and prepare lesson plans for every minute of every day. Steven D. Levitt and Stephen J. Dubner write in *Freakonomics*,

> Armed with information, experts can exert a gigantic, if unspoken, leverage: fear. . . . No one is more susceptible to an expert's fear mongering than a parent. Fear is in fact a major component of the act of parenting. A parent, after all, is the steward of another creature's life, a creature who in the beginning is more helpless than the newborn of nearly any other species. This leads a lot of parents to spend a lot of their parenting energy simply being scared. (2009, 67, 149)

Over the last few decades, early learning and public policy activists, as well as the media, have creatively overinterpreted research in brain development to the point of farce, claiming that choices made in the early years can determine everything from future parenting skills to whether a child will start smoking as a teenager. This hype has led parents and caregivers to states of paralyzing fear, forcing them to question their every choice.

All this fear burns a lot of energy. Adults deeply and truly want what is right for children, but it's difficult to know what "right" looks like. Life can be hard, and we are inclined to believe that the deceptively simple act of playing is not enough to prepare young children for its challenges. Can stacking wooden blocks or tasting mud pie really prepare a child for life? Simply saying, "Go play," seems too easy. Society has lost faith in "Go play" for a number of reasons:

- **Adults no longer trust in the idea of play.** To some extent, just goofing around with blocks, plastic cows, or construction paper seems old-fashioned. It just doesn't seem right that something so simple can prepare a child for life in the twenty-first century. To many adults, even adults who work daily with young children, play does not look like much. Play is deceptively simple. Stepping back and seeing the vast amounts of learning that come with it are difficult.

- **Parents feel pressured.** It's hard to say, "Go play," to the child in your life when the children of peers are busy all day with scheduled activities. It's easy to think that if your kid isn't enrolled in toddler kickboxing and Mandarin lessons, then he may not have a thing to talk about during his playdates with friends. What's worse, you might have a hard time explaining your choices to the other parents in your peer group. They might think you're a bad parent, and they might talk about you when you run out to the minivan for more juice boxes. Professional caregivers and parents make a lot of choices for children not because they are good choices but because everyone else has chosen it. Giving in to the pressure and following along seem easier than fighting them.

- **Adults believe learning requires teaching.** Some adults have a hard time believing that children learn when they play because they don't see any teaching happening. The idea that learning can happen without an adult taking the lead doesn't always make sense to grown-ups, in part because as children, they themselves spent much of their time in settings where an authoritative teacher attempted to fill their heads with knowledge. Their own schooling was built on a passive learning model, which makes the learning that happens during children's play hard for them to see.

Play is child-led, active learning. Two examples of how well children are able to lead their own learning through play, without adult teaching, are walking and talking.

Adults do not teach children to walk. Children learn to walk through play. From their earliest days, they build muscle strength and control as they playfully wiggle and roll, stretch and scoot. The progression from rolling, to scooting, to crawling, to pulling themselves up, to cruising along the edges of couches and toy boxes, to glorious first steps are all play centered. Little Claire reaches for a rattle and rolls over for the first time. Zeke crawls after a rolling ball. Dan pulls himself up to grab a baby doll from a shelf. Suki takes her first steps in pursuit of a playful kitten she wants to engage. Then, with persistent practice and lots more play, they eventually become toddlers, and soon after they become runners and skippers and hoppers and jumpers—again, with the help of more play. Picking up pine cones on a walk, exploring along a creek with Grandpa, chasing butterflies—all of these are playful activities that help unstable toddlers become proficient walkers. Learning to walk is a natural, play-based process that humanoids have experienced for millions of years.

Similarly, children acquire language through play. They babble to inanimate objects, take part in conversations with people and pets, play with rhymes and rhythms, create stories and play scenarios with peers, make games of building new vocabulary, and generally have fun acquiring language. The playful babbling, conversation, stories, and music we provide children are all a part of their play-based language acquisition, but we do not teach our babies to talk. They engage with their environments and lead their own playful learning. They babble, they repeat sounds, they imitate, they fashion first words and refine them, they play with syntax, they talk, and they talk, and they talk, until finally they manage to string a few words together. Then they listen and listen and listen and talk and talk and talk some more (and we talk and talk and talk back), until one day they are real human beings who will close the door if you ask or answer the phone for you if you're in the shower. It's like magic, except it's not. It's play. All of this learning unfolds through playful moments of listening, practicing, and repeating: Mommy singing silly songs and baby replying in rhythmic babbles. Daddy saying, "Who loves this baby sooooo much? Daddy does!" as he zerberts baby's belly. Grandma bursting into applause when baby toddles into the kitchen and asks for a cookie. Grandpa naming and explaining about plants and critters baby sees while strolling through the park. Play is a mind-set as much as it is an activity. This playful mind-set, an attitude open to experimentation and mistakes and full of curiosity and risk taking, is a powerful tool children use to learn language.

- **Society has made early childhood a competition.** The adult world can be very competitive. That competition has seeped into early childhood. Playing ball with the neighborhood kids in the backyard is no longer good enough. Now even young children have home and away uniforms, grown-up referees, manicured fields, training camps, and cheering fans. Parents don't just want their kids to do well; they want them to dominate the other kids. Going off to play does not have a place in these competitive settings.

- **Adults have lost touch with the way they themselves learn best.** Many adults have stagnated as learners, and their reluctance to let kids go play is due in part to their feelings about their own learning. Many grown-ups have become complacent and forgotten how much fun it is to actively engage the world. Adults get stuck in ruts and routines and aren't able to remember the magic of trying new things and learning from them.

Complete the following before moving on:

Describe how you feel when your day is dictated to you by others and you have no free time to yourself.

_____

_____

_____

_____

If you had a free afternoon this week to go play, what would you do? (Now we suggest you make some time and go play.)

_____

_____

_____

_____

What issues make it hard for you to let children go play on their own?

_____

_____

_____

_____

Falling Short

Many early learning programs have become dependent on premade curriculums that often come with detailed activity outlines and even teacher scripts. While the packaged and planned learning activities contained in these kits seem to make life easier for caregivers, they tend to fall short when compared to child-led play. Here are the problems we see with many boxed or off-the-shelf curriculums:

- They suffer from the Phoniness Factor. They do not do the real thing. They are staged, disconnected from real events, and many even provide scripts telling the caregiver what to say.

- They are unable to focus on the immediate interests of children.

- They allow adults to go on autopilot.

- They are created by people who are far removed from the children who do the learning.

- They often offer more busywork (for kids and caregivers) than active learning.

- They tend to be more product oriented than process oriented.

- They can be costly, both in terms of money and adult prep time.

- They fail to go deeply into topics, preferring to take a tourist approach that stays near the surface of subjects.

- They have a checklist mentality about learning. (Letter A, check. Number 3, check. Manners, check.)

Why the Rush?

Over a quarter of a century ago in *The Hurried Child: Growing Up Too Fast Too Soon*, David Elkind (2001, 3) wrote, "Today's child has become the unwilling, unintended victim of overwhelming stress—the stress borne of rapid, bewildering social change and constantly rising expectations." The stress and expectations have continued to mount. One caregiver we recently heard from was distressed over the intensive academic intervention a two-year-old in her care was receiving. The little girl was so overwhelmed by the well-intentioned help she was being given in response to a preschool assessment that she had begun pulling her own hair out in clumps.

Buy, Buy Baby: How Consumer Culture Manipulates Parents and Harms Young Minds, a study of the effects of consumer culture on parents and children, also attests to the hurrying of childhood. It describes what marketers refer to as "age compression" and *KGOY*—Kids Getting Older Younger. The book's author, Susan Gregory Thomas, states that while the two terms have slightly different meanings, "they both refer to the fact that today's grade-school children are dealt with the way teenagers were ten or more years ago, and so on down the age scale" (2007, 10). This means that if you are a woman over the age of about thirty-five, you probably played with Barbie and her physiologically top-heavy bosom buddies beyond the age of ten. Some of you may still have those dolls and the memories of hours of play tucked away in a box in the back of a closet. While the Barbie brand is still a cash cow, KGOY and age compression have taken a toll. Many of today's girls outgrow Barbie by age four or five, when she becomes a "baby toy."

Society loses when childhood is compressed and hurried. Many of the adults we talked to for this book feel the loss but have a hard time putting it into words. The loss is more than nostalgic warmth for long-past childhoods. At its core, it seems that many parents and professional caregivers believe the very essence of childhood is being lost. While being a kid has never been a cakewalk, historically it has been a time when the youngest among us lived unencumbered by the weight of the adult world.

It is hard to argue that children today are not pressured, stressed, pushed, exploited, sexualized, and rushed more than children were in previous generations. To some adults, this is no big deal; it's the price to be paid for living in a fast-moving, modern society. Others, however, feel that something has been left behind in the rush, and they don't fully understand why the rush is necessary.

They have a point. Think about it. Life expectancy in the United States is higher now than it ever has been. The average citizen can expect to live seventy-eight years and, unlike previous generations, can expect more of those years to be healthy and productive ones. In addition to living longer and healthier lives, our adolescence is now longer too. It's generally agreed that adolescence begins at puberty and ends at adulthood. In fact, statistics indicate that since the 1840s, puberty has set in sooner with each decade, and research shows that in the minds of most

Americans today, adulthood itself doesn't begin until sometime around a person's late twenties or early thirties. "The basic contradiction," according to Steven Mintz in *Huck's Raft: A History of American Childhood*, "is that the young are told to grow up fast, but also that they needn't grow up at all, at least not until they reach their late twenties or early thir-

ties" (2004, 381). While adolescence is expanding, childhood is compressing. Thanks to KGOY and age compression, young children today behave in the way that adolescents did a generation ago.

Back when humans were marrying at fourteen and dying of old age at forty-five, children were allowed childhoods and soon earned their keep. Now Americans live to near eighty, don't fully take on adulthood until the end of their third decade, and childhood is disappearing.

It would be nice to blame an evil cabal made up of Gargamel, Skeletor, Darth Vader, Mr. Burns, the Grinch, and the Peculiar Purple Pieman of Porcupine Peak for the theft of childhood. You can imagine them sitting in some dark hovel, plotting to steal playtime, spoil frivolity, suck fun from playrooms, cancel recess, kidnap the tooth fairy, and take away birthdays. Then, with ruthless efficiency and dark hearts, they travel the world in black helicopters, swiping toys from tots, pinching sleeping babies, and knocking over sand castles.

It would be nice to blame someone, but the only someone to blame is ourselves. We didn't do it maliciously; most of us have acted with the best of intentions. But as a society, we have collectively made choices and pursued policies that have led to the shrinking of childhood. We've brought about this rush through childhood for three reasons:

1. As a whole, Americans want the best for young children. We want them to be able to compete and succeed in the world, meeting the

challenges the future holds. We want the best for our kids, so we hurry them along. We want the best for our kids, so we expect them to perform. We want the best for our kids, so we nudge them to do just a little more. We want the best for our kids, so we drive them to succeed a bit sooner. We want the best for our kids, so we rush childhood.

2. As a whole, Americans are afraid of the unknowable future. We address this fear by rushing academics and pushing achievement. We think the best way to prepare for the scary unknown is hurriedly to cram kids full of the skills and information we think they will need. We are scared they won't have the tools to solve future problems, so we hurry them along. We are scared they will not be able to compete, so we rush them. We are scared they will be unable to meet the unknowable challenges they will encounter as adults, so we push.

3. Wanting the best for kids and fearing the future, along with honestly misunderstanding or intentionally perverting brain research, has led some to believe that hurrying children along will create superbabies. What the last few decades of neurological research have told us about raising kids, according to Steven Petersen, chief of the Neuropsychology Division at Washington University School of Medicine, is simple: "Don't raise your children in a closet, starve them, or hit them in the head with a frying pan." The Mozart Effect is a myth, Baby Einstein videos won't make kids smarter, and your baby can't read. Rushing them through childhood can actually delay development.

Wanting the best for children and hoping to allay adult fears by preparing children for the mysterious future are noble and humane goals. Every generation wants its children's lives to be happier, fuller, safer, easier, and more prosperous. Remember Gabby? Her mom, family child care provider, preschool teachers, kindergarten teacher, school administrators, and every other adult in her world wanted the best for her. Still, she lost opportunities for play and was pushed into early academics. On its surface, rushing kids along seems to be a thoughtful and good choice. It seems to be the right thing to do.

Take a moment for these questions:

How do you feel when hurried through a task you enjoy?

_____

_____

_____

Do you prefer tasks of your choosing or tasks selected by someone else? Why?

_____

_____

_____

Is Rushing Worthwhile?

Rushing childhood seems like the right thing to do, but it is not. Rushing children through their preschool years just to get them ready for kindergarten is not right. Pushing and pressuring them through kindergarten so they will be ready for first grade is not right. Hurrying, hurrying, hurrying them through first grade to prepare them for second grade is not right. Right or not, this well-intentioned rush to prepare children to succeed in life is overwhelming for them. On and on it goes, through preschool, elementary school, middle school, high school, and then college.

We rush children along with their well-being in mind, but where do we end up? According to Challenge Success (2011), an organization with whose mission is to "inform, inspire, and equip youth, parents, and schools to adopt practices that expand options for youth success," all the rushing and pressure to achieve have negative side effects:

- Over 25 percent of adolescents have felt sad or depressed every day for two or more weeks at least once during a year's time.

- Suicide is the third-largest cause of death among people between the ages of ten and twenty-four, after accidents and homicide.

- One in five students at two Ivy League colleges report purposely injuring themselves by cutting, burning, or other methods.

- Fifty-four percent of high school females and 32 percent of high school males (out of a sample of nearly five thousand Bay Area youth) reported three or more symptoms of physical stress in the past month.

- Nine- to thirteen-year-olds said they were more stressed by academics than any other stressor—even bullying or family problems.

- In a 2005 poll conducted by the *Washington Post*, the Kaiser Family Foundation, and Harvard University, 58 percent of Washington DC area adolescents surveyed said school was their biggest cause of stress.

- In a national survey, students were asked to use three words to describe how they felt in school. The words most often used by students were *bored* followed by *tired*.

- A recent McKinsey and Co. report showed that, while US fourth graders compare well on global testing, high school kids really lag. "The longer American children are in school, the worse they perform."

- Six- to eight-year-olds spend 33 percent less time playing today than in 1981.

- Kids today have twelve fewer hours of free time each week than they did in 1981.

The ever-growing body of research that Challenge Success tracks so well indicates that our desire to do right by children is actually harming them. All the pushing for success and achievement takes a toll.

What's the remedy? It seems to be that adults should back off a bit and let children have childhoods full of play. Challenge Success also reports:

- According to a study of children at more than sixty schools, by the end of fourth grade, those kids who had attended academically oriented preschools earned significantly lower grades than did those who had attended more progressive, "child-initiated" preschool classes, where the emphasis was on play.

- In Finland, kids begin formal school at age seven. While initially they score lower on tests, by age fifteen, Finnish students outperform students from every nation in reading skills. Finnish students are also among the highest scorers in math and science literacy.

Check out Challenge Success for more information on hurrying, pressuring, and rushing children.

Where Are We Rushing To?

While we rush children through childhood, we are not paying enough attention to the destination. Society is hurrying children through an eight-track cassette educational system in preparation for a post-iPod world. In fact, it is probably worse than that: the United States is preparing children for a fast-moving, postindustrial world that is driven by technology and creativity with an educational system designed back when Thomas Edison was perfecting his phonograph. This system was fine for its time, but it no longer effectively prepares children for the world they will inherit.

Algorithmic activities follow an unambiguous, step-by-step procedure for solving a problem or reaching a desired outcome. Think of tying your shoe or walking across the room. Our society used to rely heavily on routine, algorithmic work. Heuristic activities instead rely on experimentation-based, problem-solving procedures that utilize self-educating techniques. Think of a five-year-old trying to retrieve a just-out-of-reach toy car from under the couch. According to Daniel H. Pink in *Drive: The Surprising Truth about What Motivates Us*, 70 percent of job growth in the United States now comes from heuristic work.

Young children learn heuristically, and in doing so, they discover algorithms. Learning to tie your shoe—no matter how much good advice you get from caring adults—is a heuristic activity. It takes hands-on experimentation and lots of trial and error to master the skill, but once mastered, the skill integrates a shoe-tying algorithm based on the child's heuristic learning experience. Learning to walk is also a heuristic experience. It's all explorations and discovery, trial and error. Once skills are mastered, however, walking becomes a one-foot-in-front-of-the-other algorithm.

Adult-driven learning experiences tend toward the algorithmic much of the time. The assumption is that if you follow the well-planned steps, then learning will happen. But this isn't always so. You can lead a child to circle time, but you can't make her learn. The best learning experiences are heuristic in nature and depend on the child being in control of her efforts.

Our factory-model public school system is built largely on algorithms because it was designed to prepare factory workers and office drones for the industrial age. The world has changed, however, and employers do not need algorithmic workers—they need heuristic problem solvers. If you want to prepare children for the world they will inherit, send them out to play, make mistakes, and stimulate new experiences.

Sadly, our current factory-model schools could do better at helping children build the minds needed in the creativity-driven and relationship-focused world Pink foresees. In the end, our culture is rushing childhood in order to prepare kids for school curriculums that do not effectively prepare them for the world to come. Our current educational model favors logical and linear thinking over synthesizing and creative thinking, when what is needed is an educational system that educates the whole brain. Our intentions are good, but our choices should be better.

For a better understanding of why we need to educate the whole brain to prepare for the world to come, we recommend these books:

Drive: The Surprising Truth about What Motivates Us by Daniel H. Pink

A Whole New Mind: Moving from the Information Age to the Conceptual Age by Daniel H. Pink

Five Minds for the Future by Howard Gardner

The phrase "Go play" once served as the foundation of early learning. Those two simple words—shouted up stairs, across living rooms, and from open windows—led to active and engaged play, exploration, discovery, and learning. Those two words trusted children as learners and valued their time, energy, and choices. Over the last few decades, those words have been replaced with a rush toward early academics and formalized learning that has displaced play, disempowered children as leaders of their own learning, and devalued their creativity and individuality. It is time to change course and reestablish free, open, child-led, and abundant play as the primary activity of young children. It is time for an (un)curriculum.

Defining an (Un)Curriculum

My grandmother wanted me to have an education, so she kept me out of school.

—Margaret Mead, *Blackberry Winter: My Earlier Years*

In our shortsighted emphasis on testing all children and turning curriculum into test preparation (even in kindergarten), we have lost sight of the real purpose of schooling: to prepare children for the rest of their lives.

—Elizabeth Jones and Renatta M. Cooper, *Playing to Get Smart*

The rush to academics isn't working. Young children don't need a formal academic curriculum—their developing brains just aren't ready for one yet. Children need play-based learning to develop a foundation for their future academics.

If early childhood educators and parents believe that play is the most important factor in young children's learning, then they must find ways to make play a rich and frequent part of children's lives. So what's the solution to all of the rushing? What do children really need? The solution, the thing that children really need, is an (un)curriculum, and this chapter will help you understand what it is and how it works.

The word *curriculum* comes from *currere*, which is Latin for *run*. In its original Latin, the word *curriculum* means "a course"—as in a course to run around or to race a chariot around. Latin texts and ancient universities eventually began using the word to describe a formal course of academic study. Over the centuries, the word *curriculum* has worked its way from universities to high schools and then to elementary schools, preschools, and infancy. A November 2011 Google search for "infant curriculum" returned over seventy-two thousand hits. That's not many results compared to search terms like *food* or *sex*, but it does indicate the growing interest in, and availability of, formal learning materials for even the youngest among us.

Over the course of a thousand years or so, a word meaning *to run* has turned into a word that keeps children from running. A word that means *a formal course of study* has worked its way into the womb. It's kind of like the way the word *bad* sometimes means *good,* or the way *hot* and *cool* can describe the same thing. There isn't a need for a formal course of study in the womb . . .

or in the cradle . . .

or in the preschool playroom . . .

or in the kindergarten classroom.

Young children need to *currere*, but they do not need a *curriculum* telling them what to learn and when to learn it. They are entirely able and innately prepared for making those determinations on their own. Children burst into the world built to learn through their biological drive to play. Fostering play is the way to educate young children, and that requires letting them have childhoods.

Rather than a formal course of academic study, children need freedom from a formal course of academic study. They need to construct rock-solid foundations for later formal learning—through their childish pursuits. That means they need to behave in childish ways, engage in childish activities, make childish mistakes, and dream childish dreams, and they need to do it all over and over and over again, at their own pace. They need informal opportunities for hands-on play, exploration, interaction, and discovery. They need opportunities to meet the world on their own terms and at their own pace. As they discover the world, they need opportunities to discern their place in it. They need to practice being human and interacting with other humans. They need to sort, classify, and understand as they climb, manipulate, and observe.

While young children don't need a formal academic curriculum, they can't just be sent out into the world to find themselves. Little Malcolm can't be pushed out the door to fend for himself with a plastic baggie full of Cheerios in one hand and a pointy stick in the other.

Preschool-age children don't simply need adult involvement in their learning. They need the involvement of *thoughtful, caring, and interested* adults. Thoughtful, caring, and interested adults have to provide for their busy brains. They have to support their needs, physical and emotional. They have to protect children from real dangers and help them take appropriate risks. They have to let children make safe mistakes, help them travel the course children chart. Thoughtful, caring, and interested adults are the foundation of an (un)curriculum.

What an (Un)Curriculum Is Not

One effective way to understand an object or idea is to understand what it is not.

Young children invest a lot of time, energy, and brain power sorting out the world and learning to differentiate between objects. If you give a toddler a donut, then for the next two months, everything he sees that has a hole in it or a sugary taste will be a donut. Eventually he comes to understand that a bagel is not a donut, a tire is not a donut, the floaty thing in the pool is not a donut, the letter *O* is not a donut, a Danish is not a donut, a bear claw is not a donut, and the plastic stacking rings on the playroom floor are not donuts. It takes time, but learning what a donut *is not* helps kids understand what a donut *is*. Let's start defining the donut that is an (un)curriculum by investing a few hundred words in what it is not.

An (un)curriculum is not academic or formal. An (un)curriculum has little room for the worksheets, flash cards, memorization activities, lectures, and homework that inhabit the listen-up, eyes-front, keep-your-hands-to-yourself-and-your-feet-on-the-floor world.

An (un)curriculum is not Kids Gone Wild. While an (un)curriculum *is* about freedom and autonomy, it does not allow children to run wild. Developing social skills and learning self-control are important parts of an (un)curriculum.

An (un)curriculum is not the easy way out. An (un)curriculum does not free adults from the hard work of caring for children. It takes a lot of adult thought and energy to create an environment that cherishes freedom and autonomy in young children.

An (un)curriculum is not a lowering of standards. An (un)curriculum is fully dedicated to helping children become engaged, lifelong learners. An (un)curriculum carries high expectations for children.

An (un)curriculum is not something new under the sun. An (un)curriculum is based on a solid foundation of research, thinking, experience, and theory reaching back hundreds of years. Back in 1762, Rousseau published his novel *Émile, or On Education*, in which he urged a new approach to education that was based on play and respect for childhood. At its core, an (un)curriculum is an adult-supported early childhood journey.

Characteristics of an (Un)Curriculum

An (un)curriculum can be created many different ways, and good family child care providers and early childhood programs all over the world already submerse children in an (un)curriculum. The curriculum in Reggio Emilia, Italy, is an example of an (un)curriculum, as are the post–World War II British infant schools, the preschool programs at Little Red School House and Bank Street College in New York City, the Old Firehouse Schools in the Bay Area, and the Pacific Oaks Children's School in Pasadena. An (un)curriculum is specific to each place, group of children, and teacher that uses it. There are many ways to do it right.

Both of us are family child care providers, and each of us offers (un)curriculums in our programs—but our programs have lots of differences too: one program has more silly hats and cartoon characters, while the other has a larger collection of animal skulls and dead critters preserved in jars.

So, how can you tell an (un)curriculum when you see it? An (un)curriculum

- is supported by brain development research

- nurtures the individual child

- sees everything as a learning opportunity

- is based on children's needs, likes, and interests

- supports children's autonomy

- focuses on children's play

Use this list of characteristics to identify programs that practice an (un)curriculum and to assess your own.

IS SUPPORTED BY BRAIN DEVELOPMENT RESEARCH

Brain development research is the first characteristic of an (un)curriculum, because it informs all the characteristics that follow. (Un)curriculums depend on research about what brains need, how they work, and how they learn. This does not mean blindly believing every Internet newsfeed headline or every sound bite broadcast on a twenty-four-hour news station, and it certainly does not mean being taken in by "experts" selling magic superbaby beans. It means learning from reliable sources about what growing brains need.

Learning from reliable sources about what growing brains need is not always easy, however, because the sound-bite spewers and magic-bean hucksters are loud and persuasive. Not too long ago, millions of dollars were made when parents purchased Mozart CDs that were supposed to make their babies smarter. The Mozart spewers and hucksters based all their spewing and huckstering on a single successful experiment that showed college students did better on a test after listening to a bit of classical music. Other researchers could not replicate the experiment. Despite the fact that the single study looked at college brains

rather than baby brains, everyone jumped on the Mozart Effect bandwagon. Now, listening to Mozart won't do any harm, but it won't build superbabies either.

You don't have to believe us. According to *The Timing and Quality of Early Experiences Combine to Shape Brain Architecture* from the National Scientific Council on the Developing Child at Harvard University (2007, 5), "There are *no credible scientific data* to support the claim that specialized videos or particular music recordings (e.g., 'the Mozart Effect') have a positive, measurable impact on developing brain architecture." We added the italics to the quotation and will repeat the words here: "no credible scientific data to support the claim that specialized videos or particular music" have a quantifiable impact on young brains. Yet well-intended parents and caregivers spend millions on materials promising to produce superbabies. Researchers are learning more and more about how the brain functions and what it needs, but at this point, we're left with many more intriguing questions than definitive answers. As neurologist Steven Petersen says, "Don't raise your children in a closet, starve them, or hit them in the head with a frying pan." We know these three things for sure: the brain is social, the brain needs food, and the brain does not like being hit.

Brain-Based Learning

The theory of brain-based learning is built around the structure and function of the brain. Brains are not empty vessels waiting to be filled; they are active learning machines. Brains are made to learn. The theory behind brain-based learning holds that learning occurs as long as the brain is able to function normally. Twelve core principles of brain-based learning are commonly cited:

1. Brains are complex and capable of processing many different experiences, thoughts, and activities at the same time.

2. Learning engages the entire body.

3. The brain begins searching for meaning as soon as it is developed, probably before birth but certainly at birth.

4. The brain searches for meaning by creating patterns. The connections in the brain are stronger when the brain finds its own patterns.

5. Emotions are critical to creating patterns.

6. Brains process wholes and parts simultaneously. For example, a brain pays attention to information from the foreground and from the background at the same time; it processes the sand crab on the beach, the sand, the ocean, and the skyline all at once.

7. Learning involves both focused attention and peripheral perception.

8. Learning involves both conscious and unconscious processes.

9. Humans have at least two types of memory: a spatial memory system and a set of systems for rote learning.

10. The brain understands and remembers best when facts and skills are embedded in natural spatial memory.

11. Challenges enhance learning, and threats inhibit learning.

12. Each brain is unique.

These twelve principles are based on brain research conducted in the last few decades. In fact, many of these principles have been part of Montessori, Reggio Emilia, and other child-centered, play-based environments in which teachers have practiced thoughtful observation of children for generations. The push away from play toward accelerated, academic-style learning for young children has led many early learning programs away from these principles.

While knowledge about brain development can help us better understand and nurture normal development, it does not offer mechanisms for building superchildren. And many of the claims made about the brain and the importance of the first three years in a child's life lack a solid, research-based foundation. The human brain is incredibly plastic, and a child's destiny is not determined in her first three years. Some individuals and organizations have drawn conclusions and made claims that are not supported by science. Since the mid-1990s, politicians like Hillary Clinton and activists like Rob Reiner and his I Am Your Child campaign have gone a bit overboard with claims and assertions designed to influence early learning funding and public policies. Opening the April 17, 1997, White House Conference on Early Childhood Development and Learning, Mrs. Clinton claimed that experiences in the early years can "determine whether children will grow up to be peaceful or violent citizens, focused or undisciplined workers, attentive or detached parents" (quoted in Bruer 1999, 5). This is a bit of a stretch.

During the last fifteen to twenty years, the overinterpretation, twisting, and misreading of brain research to push social and political agendas have led to the normalization of early academics and the theft of childhood. The truth is that while we know the brain does not like to get hit with a frying pan, we do not know enough about the way it functions to guide public policy. And while there is a lot going on in young brains ages birth to three, we do not know enough to assert that experiences during this short window determine a child's destiny. We do know enough to help brains develop normally, but we cannot create superstudents or fix social problems during the early years. Parents and caregivers should be skeptical about such claims. To read more about this, check out *The Myth of the First Three Years: A New Understanding of Early Brain Development and Lifelong Learning* by John T. Bruer, where he writes, "Apart from eliminating gross neglect, neuroscience cannot currently tell us much about whether we can, let alone how to, influence brain development during the early stages of exuberant synapse formation" (1999, 22).

To learn more about brain-based learning and brain development, check out these resources:

Brain-Based Early Learning Activities: Connecting Theory and Practice by Nikki Darling-Kuria

Brain-Based Learning: The New Paradigm of Teaching by Eric P. Jensen

Teaching with the Brain in Mind by Eric P. Jensen

The Myth of the First Three Years: A New Understanding of Early Brain Development and Lifelong Learning by John T. Bruer

Brain-based learning is a deep subject. Read widely and deeply on the topic—not only to understand how your day-to-day practices affect children, but also so you can effectively deal with sound-bite science and magic-bean hucksters.

NURTURES THE INDIVIDUAL CHILD

Early learning is not about wooden blocks, toy trucks, baby dolls, fingerpaint, and picture books as much as it is about relationships. That is to say, it's less about the physical than the emotional environment. The brain's need for relationship drives cute little babies to connect emotionally with the people around them. Relationships are, indeed, the cornerstone of babies' learning. From these relationships grow feelings of trust, safety, predictability, belonging, and security. "Very young children can become attached to one another at an early age, and their play is more focused and successful when they are with children they have known for some time," write Margaret B. Puckett and Janet K. Black in *Understanding Toddler Development* (2007, 54). In *Understanding Infant*

Development (2007, 52), Puckett and Black write, "This developmental process is very much affected by the quality of the relationships infants form in their family and home environments, child care settings, and community."

This is true beyond infancy and toddlerhood. Relationships are important during all of childhood and throughout life. Adults learn and function better around people they know, trust, and have solid relationships with. They do better in comfortable situations. An (un)curriculum requires adult caregivers to tune in to the unique emotional needs of each child in order to build solid relationships. Adults need to be aware of children's different temperaments, learning styles, and strategies—and they need to be aware of their own stress levels.

Caregiver Stress

Programs must nurture children as individuals, but they must also nurture their staff. Have no doubt about it: stressed-out caregivers bring heavy baggage into the classroom. Managing their own stress effectively is the biggest thing caregivers who love their jobs can do to assure strong emotional environments in their classrooms. What's the biggest thing caregivers who hate their jobs can do to assure strong emotional environments—and their own happiness? Find new jobs. That may sound harsh, but children need to be surrounded by caregivers who want to be with them. Programs should seek out and hire only knowledgeable people who want to work with children. Hiring someone to work with a gaggle of toddlers or a flock of four-year-olds just because she showed up for the interview, passed a background check, and had a pulse is not enough.

For further reading on nurturing the individual child, here are our recommendations:

Your Self-Confident Baby: How to Encourage Your Child's Natural Abilities—from the Very Start by Magda Gerber and Allison Johnson

Dear Parent: Caring for Infants with Respect, 2nd edition, by Magda Gerber and Joan Weaver

The focus of these two books is infant care, but there is a lot to be learned from them even if you work with older children.

On the topic of caregiver stress and burnout, here are other books to check out:

Finding Your Smile Again: A Child Care Professional's Guide to Reducing Stress and Avoiding Burnout by Jeff A. Johnson

Keeping Your Smile: Caring for Children with Joy, Love, and Intention by Jeff A. Johnson

Now consider these questions:
How does your stress affect your relationships with the people around you?

_____

_____

_____

Describe your reaction when you find yourself in an emotional environment that feels unfriendly, hostile, or threatening.

_____

_____

_____

SEES EVERYTHING AS A LEARNING OPPORTUNITY

In an (un)curriculum, *everything* is a learning opportunity:

- feeding bugs, leeches, snails, or worms to the classroom's pet turtle

- examining rotting fruit under the playground apple tree

- talking about boogers, toenails, burps, farts, poop, scratches, and spit

- baking cookies or peeling fruit

- cutting your own hair with scissors your big sister didn't put away

- rolling a pencil back and forth across a tabletop

- picking up stones, sticks, and bugs on walks

- playing with green beans at lunch

- talking to the cashier at the grocery store

- hopping in puddles after spring rains

- paging through newspapers and catalogs

- whacking a sibling with a cardboard tube

- pushing a caregiver's buttons

- not listening to adult caregivers

All these things, and *everything* else kids do during their waking hours, are valuable learning opportunities. An (un)curriculum reaches into every nook, cranny, and crevasse of the day for real-life opportunities to support learning. Each of the moments mentioned above is a chance for caregivers to help children build on instinct and prior knowledge. Too many early childhood programs ignore these organic learning moments in favor of teacher-generated content. The big problem here is that many adults have a hard time seeing the omnipresence of learning.

They see only the learning moments that they create or that are spelled out for them in a teacher's guide. In their minds, learning takes place only when well-intended adults sit down and write lesson plans, collect materials, organize the environment, and then implement their plans.

Another reason many adults have a hard time seeing learning in moments like these is because they've been around a long time. Adults are no longer automatically excited and engaged by the silly little things that spark interest in young children. They've seen it all, been there, done that, and would buy the T-shirt if they had it in the right size and color. But seeing the depth and breadth of all the available learning opportunities requires looking through a child's eyes. It's something we all used to do instinctively, but now we need to practice to do it again.

The job of caregiver in an (un)curriculum is to see learning moments and make the most of them, building on the child's prior knowledge and life experience. Spotting learning in everyday life takes practice and requires caregivers to slow down a bit. For example, the objective of taking a walk with a troop of toddlers should not be simply to finish the walk so you can tick it off your to-do list—although this is what happens in many programs. Instead, the objective should be to slow down, experience the walk, and take advantage of the wide-reaching and often unexpected learning opportunities it offers. How often have you caught yourself saying something like "Hurry up so we can get back for lunch," or "Aaaky, put that stick down and catch up with the group," or "Say hi to the puppy and come on."

Here's an example of everything being a learning opportunity from one of our own programs:

From Jeff's World

Going on adventures is one of the most enjoyable learning activities in our family child care program—for me and for the kids. The only real difference between going on an adventure and going on a walk is that on an adventure, the kids take as much control as possible over where to go and what to do. These outings are completely unscripted, and I make every effort to make my response to their requests a resounding "Yes."

"Can we turn this way, Jeff?"

"Yes, we can."

"Can we go touch the creek?"

"Yes, but we have to climb down those rocks very carefully."

"Can we ride a bus home?"

"Yes, let's find the bus stop."

"Can I take my shoes off and step in that gooey mud?"

"Sure you can!"

"Can we touch that digger?"

"Yes, we can, if the driver says it's okay."

"Can we go on another adventure?"

"Sure."

There are no lesson plans, no predetermined learning outcomes to drive our activities, no script to follow. On these outings, our only goal is to have an adventure. Luckily, just about anything can be an adventure when you're three—things we jaded adults take for granted are fresh and new to young minds.

On a recent outing, we trespassed a few yards onto an inactive construction site and touched a huge excavator, stood in the bucket of a giant loader, and kicked the tires of a road grader. We watched welders working on a piling for a new bridge as a crane moved huge hunks of steel into place. We played with echoes under a bridge and yelled back at some grouchy redwing blackbirds. We examined a variety of random poop deposited on sidewalks, paths, and trails, decided not to touch it with our hands, poked some of it with sticks, and discussed its origins, consistency, and texture. We also followed a big brown cricket across a sidewalk and into the grass, tossed rocks into a creek and watched the splashes and ripples they made, got muddy and hot and then sat in the shade of a huge maple tree, visited two playgrounds where we took turns on the equipment and talked to strangers, cheered for a robin as it wrestled a worm from the ground and devoured it, cheered for a worm as it inched from an exposed position on a wet sidewalk to the much safer cover of dirt and grass, watched water plummet over six amazing and loud "waterfalls," and stopped to watch "quiet water" at four or five different locations, comparing its lack of sound to the noise of those wild, splashy "waterfalls."

We weren't done yet. We also experienced a wide variety of bugs, trees, plants, people, buildings, surfaces, textures, sounds, and smells; rushed, sauntered, strutted, strolled, toddled, stumbled, climbed, slipped, balanced, wobbled, teetered, and tottered along; overcame two scraped knees, a scraped palm, and a little cut, none of them life threatening, all of them educational; and headed back to the house hungry, tired, and full of new experiences.

Our adventure experiences become a major part of the conversations and play that the children engage in for days afterward. These sensory-rich and hands-on experiences stuck in their brains.

Try these books to learn more about seeing and making the most of the learning opportunities that are all around you:

Teaching by Heart by Mimi Brodsky Chenfeld

Creative Experiences for Young Children by Mimi Brodsky Chenfeld

The Art of Awareness: How Observation Can Transform Your Teaching by Deb Curtis and Margie Carter

Now take a few moments to consider the following:

What parts of the world spoke to you the clearest when you were a child?

_____

_____

_____

Describe the last time you felt tuned in to your surroundings. Where were you? What were you doing? Why were you able to tune in then?

_____

_____

_____

Find a place you can be alone for ten minutes. Sit comfortably and close your eyes for a few moments. When you open them, make a list of all the things you see.

_____

_____

_____

_____

_____

_____

_____

_____

Use the list you just made to think of ways you could use what you observed to engage children in play.

_____

_____

_____

_____

_____

_____

_____

_____

IS BASED ON CHILDREN'S NEEDS, LIKES, AND INTERESTS

Most early learning programs claim to be child centered, and while many are, many more morph from child centered to adult centered: over-time, schedules, activities, room arrangements, menus, and everything else are transformed to make life easier for the adults. For example, the frequency of outside play often decreases, because getting kids ready to go outside is a hassle, and cleaning up the mess tracked in after play is no fun either. Varied menus are often replaced with the same-old-same-old because it's cheaper and simpler to prepare. In an (un)curriculum, great care is taken to ensure that all aspects of the program are geared to the unique needs of the children. This doesn't mean adult needs are cast aside and ignored; after all, children need happy, contented, and comfortable caregivers. It simply means a continuous, concerted effort is made to keep physical and emotional environments tuned to the needs of the children in them.

Children are complex, unique, and multifaceted, and they need learning environments that take these characteristics into consideration. Children should be given what they need when they need it, not when a calendar, lesson plan, or curriculum guide says they should get it. Just because a teacher's guide says this is bug week does not mean little Jenny is ready to learn about bugs. Planning must bend and flex to the needs of the individual children in the program, and an (un)curriculum works to meet the needs of the *whole* child, not just the kindergarten-readiness or standardized-tests parts. Young children are more than their future reading and math scores. Besides, research tells us that kids who engage in an (un)curriculum do better academically in the end. New research from Alison Gopnik's lab in Berkeley and from Massachusetts Institute of Technology is the latest to show that young children learn more and more deeply from self-directed exploration than from being "taught." Gopnik concludes a March 2011 Slate.com article on this topic with these words: "It's more important than ever to give children's remarkable, spontaneous learning abilities free rein. That means a rich, stable, and safe world, with affectionate and supportive grown-ups, and lots of opportunities for exploration and play. Not school for babies" (www.slate.com/id/2288402/). A caregiver cannot interrupt the flow of a child's interest-driven play to teach something prescribed by a lesson plan *and* sustain a child-centered program.

A truly child-centered program should include these five elements:

1. Low turnover: staff are happy with their jobs and stay with their programs for long periods of time.

2. Primary caregivers: one caregiver is responsible for the majority of the care of a specific child and therefore builds a strong and trusting relationship with him.

3. Continuity of care: a group of children stay with the same caregiver(s) for an extended period of time in order to build strong emotional relationships.

4. Small group size: caregivers are responsible for a small number of children, and the overall number of children in a room is low.

5. Mixed-ability groups: children spend their days with kids of different ages and developmental levels.

While these five elements should be present in a child-centered program, they are not mandatory, and their presence does not guarantee that the program is a child-centered or quality one. Many very child-centered Montessori programs don't have low ratios or small group sizes, for example, and neither do the Reggio programs in Italy. Similarly, some programs employ methods other than primary caregiving to make sure children build strong relationships. It is perfectly possible for programs to lack in one or more of these five elements and still offer truly child-centered programs. It is possible to do right by young children using practices that buck early learning orthodoxy.

These five elements of a truly child-centered program will be explained further in chapter 3. They are important to child-centeredness because they help ensure that individual children are securely attached to their caregivers and that they have opportunities to learn from and teach their peers.

SUPPORTS CHILDREN'S AUTONOMY

In *Drive*, Daniel H. Pink writes, "Human beings have an innate inner drive to be autonomous, self-determined, and connected to one another. And when that drive is liberated, people achieve more and live richer lives" (2009, 71). Long before Pink wrote *Drive*, Thomas Aquinas wrote, "The highest manifestation of life consists in this: that a being governs its own actions. A thing which is always subject to the direction of another is somewhat of a dead thing."

Pink believes that adults should have autonomy over four aspects of their work:

- Tasks (what you do)

- Time (when you do it)

- Techniques (how you do it)

- Team (who you do it with)

We contacted Pink after reading this in *Drive*, and he agreed that his four Ts could be extended to play, which is the work of children (February 1, 2010). When designing learning activities, projects, and play opportunities, allow children autonomy over their Tasks, Time, Techniques, and Team. (We will look more at these four Ts in chapter 4, where we discuss planning.)

Some other smart people have said the following about the importance of autonomy:

> They [the makers of the Constitution] conferred, as against the government, the right to be let alone—the most comprehensive of rights and the right most valued by civilized men.
>
> —Supreme Court Justice Louis D. Brandeis,
>   *Olmstead v. U.S.* (1928)

> Growth and mastery come only to those who vigorously self-direct. Initiating, creating, doing, reflecting, freely associating, enjoying privacy—these are precisely what the structures of schooling are set up to prevent, on one pretext or another.
>
> —John Taylor Gatto, *The Underground History*
>   *of American Education*

Listen to the desires of your children. Encourage them and then give them the autonomy to make their own decision.

—Denis Waitley, author and motivational speaker

Our treatment of both older people and children reflects the value we place on independence and autonomy. We do our best to make our children independent from birth. We leave them all alone in rooms with the lights out and tell them, "Go to sleep by yourselves." And the old people we respect most are the ones who will fight for their independence, who would sooner starve to death than ask for help.

—Margaret Mead, Introduction to "Growing Old in America" by Grace Hechinger, *Family Circle*, July 25, 1977.

Our belief that children benefit as learners from autonomy is, in part, based on Self-Determination Theory (SDT), which proposes that people possess innate tendencies to behave in ways that are healthy and beneficial. Developed by Edward L. Deci and Richard M. Ryan at the University of Rochester, the theory has been expanded and refined by scholars and researchers around the world. You can learn more about SDT by visiting www.psych.rochester.edu/SDT/.

There is a lot of talk in the early learning world about the need to empower children, to give them the power to grow, learn, and thrive. This assumes that the power to do these things is in the hands of adults and that adults are able to dispense them in measured doses. In reality, we are all born with the power and drive to learn. We do not empower children to walk or talk; these processes are innate and autonomously driven. Children do not learn to walk and talk for other people; they do it for their own well-being and survival. While we have no power to give children, we surely can support their autonomous inclinations and nurture their drive to know the world. Supporting autonomy is not difficult. It can be as simple as waiting the few minutes it takes a two-year-old to put on her own shoes instead of doing it for her because doing so is easier and quicker, or letting a group of three-year-olds decide how they want to spend their outside time on a beautiful spring morning instead of planning an activity for them.

When children are allowed autonomy over Pink's four Ts (Tasks, Time, Technique, and Team), all the activities they engage in will be powerful learning moments, because the moments will be developmentally relevant and interest driven. When we asked Peter Gray in an e-mail what part children should play in determining what they learn, when they learn it, and how the learning happens, he responded, "They should be completely in charge of all of this. Truly, nobody can do it for them. Nature has created children to be little learning machines— but the machinery only works when they are in charge."

Take some time to dig into the following:

Share a moment when you felt in control of your tasks, time, technique, and team.

_____

_____

_____

Share a moment when you had your tasks, time, technique, and team dictated to you by an authority figure.

_____

_____

_____

Which moment brings back the most positive memories? What part of the moment left you with those good memories?

_____

_____

_____

FOCUSES ON CHILDREN'S PLAY

The last piece of our (un)curriculum puzzle is an unwavering commitment to play. Brains need play, and play is the obvious antidote to rushing children through childhood. *A commitment to play is the defining feature of an (un)curriculum.*

Stuart Brown, a play researcher who frequently consults with large companies interested in learning how to improve employee creativity through play, writes, "Of all animal species, humans are the biggest players of all. We are built to play and built through play. When we play, we are engaged in the purest expression of our humanity, the truest expression of our individuality" (2009, 5).

An (un)curriculum instills a passion for play in adults and children. It encourages people to play with materials, ideas, language, choices, and all the rest of life in an effort to gain understanding and refine knowledge. An (un)curriculum is even more than play based—it's play obsessed.

Consider the following:

Describe the last time you felt playful in your adult life. What brought about this feeling? How did it make you feel? What did you learn from the experience?

_____

_____

_____

Think back to a favorite play activity from your childhood. What did you learn through that play that's still with you as an adult?

_____

_____

_____

Make a list of the activities that the children in your life find most engaging. How playful are these activities? Who initiates them? Is any learning taking place?

_____

_____

_____

In your own effort to know more about the importance of play in the lives of children, try these books—they're a great starting point.

Play: How It Shapes the Brain, Opens the Imagination, and Invigorates the Soul by Stuart Brown with Christopher Vaughan

Play = Learning: How Play Motivates and Enhances Children's Cognitive and Social-Emotional Growth, edited by Dorothy G. Singer, Roberta Michnick Golinkoff, Kathy Hirsh-Pasek

The Power of Play: Learning What Comes Naturally by David Elkind

The (un)curriculum outlined here is a back-to-basics approach that when implemented looks a lot like the childhoods many adults had. It offers freedom to play, to engage the world, and to explore.

Push the Curriculum Back Up

Our current educational system tends to look at what children are expected to know and achieve down the road and then pushes them at ever-younger ages in the direction of those skills. After all, kids have to learn to read in elementary school, so why not get them started reading in preschool? If we teach a six-year-old's skill to a four-year-old, then we're doing a good thing, because he'll be more advanced, right? These beliefs have led to "curriculum creep"—kids doing things in preschool that used to be part of a first-grade curriculum.

The problem is that preschoolers are not first graders and four-year-olds are not six-year-olds. Their brains are fundamentally different. A child needs to build four-year-old skills and experiences before she can become a six-year-old and learn six-year-old stuff. Don't look into the future to determine your curriculum. Instead, look right in front of you. Focus on what kids in your care need right now, in this very moment. This is the best way to prepare for the future.

Have the courage to push the curriculum back up. Make play the center of early childhood and let kids be kids. Allow them their silliness. Let them play, explore, and discover their worlds at their own pace, in their own way.

Here are some tips to help you fight the good fight:

- **Keep learning.** Stay on top of the research and keep informed about legislation and policies affecting early learning. Don't just gobble the sound bites on the evening news—dig deeper.

- **Speak up**. Change comes when strong voices speak up and demand change. Share your knowledge and experience with parents, peers, and leaders on local, state, and national levels.

- **Live it.** If you believe we are rushing childhood, you should do everything you can to become an agent of change. Live your beliefs. Make sure the children in your care get to be children. Talking about the importance of play and childhood is not the same as making play important in your day-to-day life.

In review, programs offering an (un)curriculum make choices based on brain development research; nurture individual children; see everything as a learning opportunity; base planning choices on children's needs, likes, and interests; support children's autonomy; and focus on real, hands-on children's play. A primary goal of such programs is to push formalized academic curriculums out of early childhood education and slow the rush of childhood. This is not an easy endeavor, and programs willing to take it on need support—which is the topic of the next chapter.

Supporting an (Un)Curriculum

We want our children to know how to find the right answer when there is one, but we also want them to be able to think outside the box. Where does creativity come from? From play—good old unmonitored, unrestricted free and open play.

> —Kathy Hirsh-Pasek and Roberta Michnick Golinkoff, Einstein, *Never Used Flash Cards: How Our Children Really Learn—and Why They Need to Play More and Memorize Less*

What's in greatest demand today isn't analysis but synthesis—seeing the big picture, crossing boundaries, and being able to combine disparate pieces into an arresting new whole.

> —Daniel H. Pink, *A Whole New Mind: Why Right-Brainers Will Rule the Future*

Now you know what an (un)curriculum looks like. It typically has these primary characteristics:

- An (un)curriculum is supported by brain-development research.

- An (un)curriculum nurtures each individual child.

- An (un)curriculum sees everything as a learning opportunity.

- An (un)curriculum is based on children's needs, likes, and interests.

- An (un)curriculum supports children's autonomy.

- An (un)curriculum is focused on children's play.

But what does it take to create an environment that supports an (un)curriculum on a programmatic level? What steps can you take to transform your program? This chapter is devoted to seeing ways early learning programs can support an (un)curriculum through thoughtful policies and practices. Our goal is to help you take a fresh look at your program's foundations and think about how they influence your interactions with children. You may find that these foundations are deep and strong, or you may find that some thoughtful changes over time are necessary.

Seven programming guidelines make an (un)curriculum possible:

1. Trust your employees.

2. Focus on art.

3. Truly value play.

4. Encourage activist caregivers.

5. Overcome fear.

6. Seek out simplicity.

7. Value vacation mind-sets.

Trust Your Employees

The first concrete step your program can take to support an (un)curriculum is to enact policies and practices demonstrating that employees are truly trusted. Trust is key to early learning. "Absolutely critical to children's well-being, a sense of security is rooted in the trust that babies develop from the first days of life when they learn that they can count on their caretakers," writes Nancy Carlsson-Paige (2008, 11) in *Taking Back Childhood: A Proven Roadmap for Raising Confident, Creative, Compassionate Kids*. From their earliest days and throughout their early years, children need caregivers they can trust, which means programs must hire only trustworthy people. Programs that inherently distrust the same caregivers that children rely on to build secure and trusting relationships are dysfunctional at their core.

Really Trusting Caregivers

It's unfortunate that most programs implicitly or explicitly convey a lack of trust in their caregivers' competence as well as a pessimistic prediction about their caregivers' future behavior.

States and organizations have piles of policies and reams of regulations written and implemented under the guise of protecting children and assuring safety. But the truth is that many of these rules and regulations function at least in part as flak jackets to protect the Powers That Be. One of the first things to go through the mind of a program director, principal, human services director, or state legislator when she hears of a child being injured, abused, or killed on her watch is "Phew! I'm covered. We have a policy about that." And on the off chance that there isn't a self-protective policy in place, you can rest assured one will soon be written and implemented.

Sometimes these "protect my posterior" policies aren't even written down. For example, over the last few years, Jeff has spoken with at least half a dozen center directors who candidly stated that while they think there should be more men working in child care, they refuse to hire them in their programs because, as one director put it, "It's just too dangerous; something could happen, and I would be to blame." When pressed about what kind of "something" she was referring to, the director replied, "You know, some perverted sex thing."

Now to be fair, self-protection is not the sole reason many policies, rules, and regulations hit the books or are implemented off the books. The people imposing them have good intentions and

truly want children to be safe, but self-protection surely plays an important part in the rule making.

As it should. If you've been anywhere near the field of early care and education for more than a year or two, then you know that a small percentage of people working in the profession have no business being around young children. They

are not professional, they do not feel caregiving is their calling, and they lack training and natural ability. Some of them are just happy to have a job, even one they're not keen on. Some people work in the child care profession simply because a program interviewed them and the pizza place around the corner wouldn't. You probably know caregivers who fall into these categories. Sadly, a tiny percentage of these people—men and women—probably are looking for opportunities to do "perverted sex things" with young children, so if you are in any position of authority, protecting your posterior is prudent.

What do we mean when we say "trustworthy people"? Here's a definition of trust that we find helpful: "Trust is an essential belief in and reliance on the competence of another; it is an internal state that is built through person-person experience. Trust entails expectation, a prediction about how someone will behave, and since it is future oriented, it is predicated on optimism" (Marano 2008, 191). This is the kind of trust in caregivers that is essential to the creation of an (un)curriculum.

Caregivers should be fully trusted to make good choices, behave mindfully, and act in the best interest of children at all times. But all the rules, regulation, policies, and monitoring—and the paperwork that comes with them—can weigh heavily on staff and lead good people to feel micromanaged, belittled, disrespected, and mistrusted. They can also scare administrators, leaving them worrying more about liability than about learning. From the very beginning of their employment, many professionals feel as if they are already presumed guilty of some wrong. One fresh and bubbly recent graduate we spoke with was happy to find a well-paying job where she could put her early childhood education degree to work, but she felt disenchanted after her orientation. "The whole day was about 'Don't do this'; 'You can't do that'; 'Never *ever* do this,'" she told us. "It felt more like I was being coached on how to avoid being shivved in the yard on my first day in prison than on how to work with children. I was actually told, 'Hugs are dangerous. Avoid them.' I almost didn't go back." A lack of trust can have a direct and palpable impact on the overall quality of a program and the types of learning activities its caregivers provide.

When you don't feel trusted, you don't feel respected. You also second-guess yourself and struggle to trust your own instincts, skills, and training. A lack of trust can have a direct and palpable impact on a program's overall quality as well as on the kinds of learning activities its caregivers provide. One day of these feelings was almost enough to scare that young graduate away from her dream job—and just try to imagine being a man working in a program where his intentions are always under suspicion. In *Linchpin: Are You Indispensable?* Seth Godin writes, "Let me be really clear: Great teachers are wonderful. They change lives. We need them. The problem is that most schools don't like great teachers. They're organized to stamp them out, bore them, bureaucratize them, and make them average" (2010, 29). It's our opinion that this effort to stamp out greatness starts with a lack of trust.

Here's a recap:

- Some people working in this field have no business being around children.

- Too many dedicated professionals feel beaten down because they aren't respected or trusted.

- Many administrators and policy makers are overcautious and concerned with self-protection when it comes to implementing rules and regulations.

Here are five suggestions for developing an atmosphere in which employees feel trusted:

1. Help people working in the profession who do not possess the skills, temperament, or inclination to be early learning professionals to find employment in fields that suit their skills, temperaments, and inclinations. The early learning profession will be better off without them, and they will be more fulfilled doing something they are called to.

2. Implement trust-based rules and regulations to fully support the dedicated women and men who give themselves to this profession. Replace policies that bully, badger, belittle, and besiege with policies that build up and empower.

3. Don't impose blanket polices to address the behavior of one incompetent employee. A restrictive new dress code for the entire staff in response to Mandy's wearing low-rise short shorts and too-small tube tops punishes the sensible dressers for one person's lack of sense.

4. When creating policies and procedures for your program, assume that your staff members are competent and have good judgment. If they are not competent or do not have good judgment, then they should not be working with children. Deal with incompetent employees directly.

5. Never, ever hire people into this profession simply because they are warm bodies. Hire only people with commitment, training, and innate skill—people you can fully trust. If being able to trust them

means a forty-hour preservice training course, fine. If it means a six-month probationary apprenticeship before becoming a full staff member, fine. If it means pairing them with experienced mentors for the first two years in the field, fine. The value of interpersonal trust cannot be overrated. If you do not trust them, do not hire them.

Check out these books related to this topic:

Seth Godin's *Linchpin: Are You Indispensable?*

Daniel H. Pink's *Drive: The Surprising Truth about What Motivates Us*

Focus on Art

Once your program is staffed with people you truly trust, make sure your policies and practices treat them like Artists, not Cogs. You have to respect the talents and unique skills they bring to the job. Do everything you can to remind staff members of these seven words:

I Am an Artist, Not a Cog.

Hang them on the bathroom mirror, print them on note cards employees can keep in their purses or billfolds, mount them in fancy frames above changing tables or kitchen sinks, add them to your Facebook profile and website, or go on a staff field trip so everyone can have them tattooed on their forearms: *I Am an Artist* on the left arm, *Not a Cog* on the right arm.

These seven words and the mind-set that accompanies them have a direct and vital impact on the lives caregivers live and the care they provide.

Artists think and act differently than Cogs. Artists work to master technique, have passion for their work, feel called to their art, bring emotion to the endeavor, and frequently exhaust themselves physically and spiritually in pursuit of their craft. In *Linchpin*, Seth Godin defines artists as "people with a genius for finding a new answer, a new connection, or a new way of getting things done" (Godin 2010, 8). Cogs go through the motions. They whiz and they whir, spinning frantically or

56

clicking along methodically, but never going anywhere. Cogs are interchangeable and replicable. Cogs break down and wear out.

If you think for a moment that consistently meeting the physical, social, and emotional needs of children is not an artist's work, you need to think for another moment or two. Children are not interchangeable products rolling along a high-speed factory assembly line; they are as unique as the genes they've inherited and the moments they've lived. Nurturing these precious individuals takes heart, passion, emotional labor, patience, skills, drive, and dedication.

We all prefer interacting with people who bring these things to their work. Think about it:

- Do you prefer a meal prepared by a fast-food assembly line or by someone who loves to cook?

- Do you prefer having your hair done by a technically proficient stylist or by a creative stylist who has mastered technique?

- Do you prefer a cashier at the grocery store who simply pushes the right buttons or one who offers a genuine smile, connects to you as a fellow human being, and cares enough not to put the five-pound bag of flour on top of the loaf of bread?

- Do you fondly remember the teacher who scolded you for daydreaming or the one who inspired you to make something of those dreams?

- If you were a child, would you prefer a caregiver who is a Cog or an Artist?

Current policies and regulations governing teachers and other professional caregivers keep the Cogs spinning, but do not inspire and support the Artists. The problem with this is that the best Cog in the world is still a Cog. Caregivers and teachers exhausted by heavy-handed regulations have little energy left for the important emotional labor that is the core of the job—the place where much of the Art happens.

Teachers and child care providers choke on red tape and strangle on arbitrary rules and regulations that, although well-intentioned, force them into the role of Cog and squeeze off their Artist instincts. Rules and regulations are written with the intent of making the worst of the Cogs less bad instead of helping the Artists shine. They try to make everything black or white, implementing policies meant to standardize procedures and practices and eliminate shades of gray. The reality is that no matter how hard you try, it is impossible to devise a rigid set of rules, policies, and procedures that will assure quality; caring for and educating young children is not the same as building a Model T. Early learning programs desperately need policies and practices that help caregivers and teachers shine while they nurture and educate children, because early learning is not the kind of black-and-white work that the Cogs do well.

Let us repeat those seven words: *I Am an Artist, Not a Cog.*

Here are a few concrete ways to support caregivers as Artists:

- **Hold fewer meetings.** Let's face it: most meetings are boring, don't accomplish anything, and numb the mind. We all know that the real decisions are made before the meetings start or in the hallway just after. If you can say it in an e-mail, send an e-mail. Don't make the whole staff sit and listen to a policy lecture that is directed at a single person. Talk *with* staff members instead of talking *at* them. Have real conversations instead of lecturing.

- **Look at training as an opportunity to support personal growth.** Look for training and mentoring opportunities that engage caregivers and allow them to stretch professionally. Don't view training simply an opportunity to collect the right number of certificates for each employee's personnel file each year.

- **Support those doing direct care with real breaks and regular planning time.** Watching the nappers or folding towels is not a break, and scribbling on a calendar while a flock of two-year-olds climbs you is not planning time. Caregivers need to get out of the classroom for breaks and for planning time. This may mean the director needs to spend time in the classroom giving breaks or covering during planning time.

- **Include existing staff in the hiring process.** If the new hire is going to work in the infant room, then the current infant staff should have a huge amount of input into who gets hired, because they will have to work closely with her.

- **Give staff as much ownership of the program as possible**. Involve them in policy making, budgeting, long-range planning, and all the other ins and outs of your program.

- **Go through your employee handbook and cut out anything written for Cogs.** In *The Story Factor: Inspiration, Influence, and Persuasion Through the Art of Storytelling*, Annette Simmons writes, "Mandatory rules don't allow participation and tend to influence people to either mindless obedience or gleeful malicious obedience that can actually make things worse" (2006, 527). Too many rules and policies aimed at controlling and keeping Artists in line can turn them into rebels.

- **Create spaces and policies that support Artists.** This may include such things as a child-free break room where staff can unwind, planning time, vacation and sick days, control over their four Ts (Tasks, Time, Techniques, and Team), a key to the supply cabinet, and a trust-based work environment.

Truly Value Play

If your program brochure and advertisements say you offer hands-on, play-based learning, then you should offer hands-on, play-based learning. It seems like common sense, but many programs talk a good game about the value of play and then fail to walk that talk in their program's actual practices. If your (un)curriculum is to thrive, then you have to make sure your actions support the words in your program's marketing materials as well as the words that come out of your mouth when you talk about your program. One program we've encountered devotes a great deal of its website space to talking about the value of play, but in reality, it has three-year-olds sitting in chairs doing worksheets for much of the day. Programs that embrace an (un)curriculum need to value play as a core tenet of their existence. They cannot just talk the talk. Here are some things to consider when looking at your policies and practices:

- **Look at your schedule.** Are large hunks of the day set aside for free play? Do children get to choose how they spend their time? Consider changes that build more time for play into the day. For example, if your posted schedule is broken into a bunch of short blocks of time (music time, circle time, craft time, and so on) you could combine those blocks and allow each of the children to choose the activity they want to engage in. Another option would be to provide a wide variety of interesting materials and then say two of our favorite words: *Go play!*

- **Look at your practices.** Do you use a lot of worksheets and flash cards? Are kids forced to take part in activities they are not interested in? Do you focus on early academics? Consider revising your practices so you don't use worksheets and flash cards; children choose most or all of their activities; and play rather than academics is the focus of each day. This can be a very scary proposition if you've never done it before—just thinking about it leaves some caregivers worried, fretful, and twitchy—but in our experience, children allowed to lead their own play are more focused and better behaved. The children in the care of one caregiver we know ripped her collection of flash cards and worksheet masters into tiny pieces and added them to the compost pile. Once the offending materials were out of hand, they were also out of mind, and it became easier for her to transition to play-based policies and practices.

- **Read up on play.** The suggested reading and websites we pulled together at the back of this book are a good place to start. For updates and more ideas, check out this link too: www.facebook.com/LetThemPlayBook.

Encourage Activist Caregivers

Caregivers too often passively accept well-intentioned but impractical, developmentally inappropriate, or downright inane policies, practices, regulations, and dictates handed down to them or thrust upon them by the Powers That Be. It's our opinion that professional caregivers need to become activists against things they believe hinder developmentally appropriate learning, impede play, and steal childhood. Over the last few decades, play has been incrementally squeezed out of the lives of children and replaced with a rigid academic focus. This has happened because not enough people have stood up and made a ruckus about the changes; it has been easier to keep our heads down. The thing is, children need adults in their lives who are willing to stand up and actively fight against the push to steal childhood. They need activist caregivers and programs with policies and practices that support such caregivers.

Being an activist caregiver means standing up for your program, your beliefs, and your way of doing things. Rocking the boat can be scary, but in the end it's the only way we can protect play and childhood.

While doing research for this book, we heard about one program that decided not to use its brand-new water play tables—or engage in any kind of water play, for that matter. On their last licensing visit, they were told that only one child at a time could play at a table, using no more than half an inch of water. They were also told the water play station had to be emptied, disinfected, and refilled between each child's play. While the state regulation wasn't actually this stringent, the state employee responsible for issuing licenses had imposed her own standards. To be safe and to avoid licensing problems, the program did away with water play.

Another program ended a long-running partnership with a nearby senior center. The children would periodically visit the seniors at the center, and when they did, the seniors would read to the children and rock the babies on a volunteer basis. The reason for ending the partnership? Potential liability, in case one of the grandmas or grandpas misbehaved.

A family child care provider was written up for a possible choking hazard: a garden hose, on a reel, attached to the side of her house. The person evaluating the provider was afraid a child might wrap it around her own neck and choke to death. And while this could happen, in the whole history of garden hoses, it probably hasn't.

Scenarios like these are not uncommon. One of the best things caregivers can do to counteract the policies and mind-sets that create them is to speak up and get actively involved in the creation and implementation of early learning regulations and policies on local, state, and national levels. Caregivers should share their stories about the laws, regulations, and practices that get in the way of making good choices for children with decision makers in their programs as well as on the state and national levels. Speaking up is the only way early childhood professionals can have influence and bring about change. Sharing your stories, ideas, and opinions through social media and with parents is another concrete way to actively fight for play and childhood. Address your concerns directly to any officials who visit your program, and if they do not come to visit you, make an effort to seek them out in person or online. If you don't agree with something a licensor, meal program representative, health department official, or fire inspector tells you to do or writes you up for, then ask for clarification, have a discussion, defend your choices, or request to see the written regulation being referred to. Don't be disrespectful, but don't be scared or intimidated either.

As an activist caregiver, look for opportunities to connect with other like-minded caregivers. Many voices speaking together can be very powerful. You can connect with us, too, at www.explorationsearlylearning .com (Jeff) and www.playcounts.com (Denita).

Overcome Fear

Programs often enact policies and practices out of fear. Administrators and decision makers somehow think that having lots of polices and rules makes programs immune to danger, that programs are safer if only they can write a rule or policy to cover everything that could possibly go wrong. The problem with this thinking is that every unexpected possibility cannot be planned for. That's why the unexpected is such a surprise when it happens. Fear-based policies and practices can get in the way of play and the implementation of an (un)curriculum.

Consider these five points about fear and danger:

1. While there are real dangers in the world, our contention is that unfounded fear and perceived danger influence adult choices so much that they have a negative impact on early learning. We believe that as a society, our fear outweighs the real threats—people see more danger than really exists—and we let these things cloud our judgment when it comes to children.

2. Concerned adults need to keep overstimulated fear glands in check, step back a few paces, and trust children a bit. This does not mean we advocate abandoning small children to fend for themselves; the last thing we want is mobs of hungry, drooling toddlers roaming the streets in sagging diapers, searching for neat things to stick up their noses.

3. Adults' bubbling-just-below-the-surface fear and constant eyeballing are stealing childhood. Today's children have lost much of the autonomy—over their time, energy, and resources—that past generations had because so many adults in charge are just about to boil over with fear.

4. Real play—and real learning—sometimes comes with real bumps, real bruises, real hurt feelings, real skinned knees, real ruffled emotions, and moments of real fear. Invite these real things into your learning environment and celebrate, rather than avoid, them. People learn to deal with real-world danger and fear by experiencing them, not by trying to regulate them out of existence (something that is impossible to do). Play offers a safe environment for this learning. We agree with the words of Stuart Brown: "The fact is that play is not completely without cost. Play can be dangerous" (2009, 49).

5. Fearful adults create fearful children. This cycle must be broken, or eventually there will be no one left to escort scary spiders from bathtubs, investigate what makes those thumps in the dark, or stand up and speak in front of crowds.

Some modern children never leave the sight of a caring and concerned adult, one who believes overmonitoring is justified because life is so dangerous. Even when children think they are alone, it's common for someone to be watching—there are audio and video monitors to watch kids while they sleep, GPS tracking devices to track their every move, and child care center webcams and teddy bears with built-in spy cameras to watch the people who are watching children. On top of all that, many, if not most, states require that caregivers in child care and preschool programs have direct view of all children at all times. This makes the refrigerator-box clubhouse and the draped sheet tent that were part of many adults' childhoods illegal in many early care and learning programs. For a kid, this fear and hypersurveillance mean at least four things:

- Rich, learning-filled private play disappears from your day.

- A well-intentioned adult is always eyeballing you, so you acquire a limited concept of privacy.

- You learn to be fearful and worried because the adults around you seem to be fearful and worried.

- With an adult always in sight, you have limited opportunities to solve your own problems, make your own rules, and build your own identity.

Relentless monitoring takes an emotional toll. Think about the last time you found yourself driving down the road and noticed a police car cruising behind you. You're on your way to buy milk and bananas, but for a moment, you feel guilty—like you just robbed a bank. You tense up a bit, put down your cell phone or mascara, take your foot off the gas pedal, check to see if your seat belt is on, and reassure yourself that your registration, proof of insurance, and license are in the car with you. In that moment, you feel guilty of something just because an authority figure is nearby. You feel you have to be on your best behavior, that you have to change your conduct to avoid trouble. Instead of watching the road, you're thinking, "Sorry, officer, I was going to buy bananas, but I will never do it again. I swear! Can you just let me off with a warning?"

Kids feel the same way when adults don't trust them to go out of our sight and constantly monitor their every mannerism, movement, and mood—even when we tell them we are doing it for their own good. Children need appropriate supervision, not constant, fear-based supervision. Here are some tips for creating a less fearful early learning setting:

- **Create private spaces for children.** Remember how as a kid you would build a fort under the kitchen table or behind the couch, or how you would pull the blankets over your head and read with a flashlight, or hide in the branches of a large spruce tree? Remember the privacy, the calm focus of being alone, the sneaky feeling as you peeked out into the world from your private hideaway? Kids in early learning programs need these private spaces, and we should work to provide them.

- **Look for loopholes and ways around some of the regulated fear.**
  Are there procedural things you can do to make some forbidden
  forms of play allowable?

- **Take a lower score.** Many of the rules and regulations that make
  child care such a fearful place come from voluntary rating scales. The
  thing is, you can choose to take a lower score on a particular standard in order to bring a little vitality and excitement back to play.
  We'd rather run a program where kids can play in a tub of water
  together or climb the apple tree than one where we forbid those
  things in order to get an extra star on a certificate.

Seek Out Simplicity

There is growing evidence that when it comes to early learning, less is more. Simple toys, like blocks, sand, and empty cardboard boxes, have been found to increase child-directed play more than fancy, bright, beeping, buzzing toys based on cartoon characters or television shows. Unscheduled free time can be more valuable for learning and mental health than involvement in lots of adult-organized activities. Time away from computers, video games, televi-sion, and other technologies is more educational than time glued in front of these things. "The problem with computers isn't computers—they're just tools," writes Richard Louv in *Last Child in the Woods: Saving Our Children from Nature-Deficit Disorder.* "The problem is that overdependence

on them displaces other sources of education, from the arts to nature. As we pour money and attention into educational electronics, we allow less fashionable but more effective tools to atrophy" (2008, 137).

Programs working to build (un)curriculums should seek out simplicity instead of looking for ways to make childhood more complicated. Here are some concrete tips for implementing policies and practices that support an (un)curriculum:

- **Think old school.** Look back at learning spaces and materials from the past and make them a part of your program. There is a reason empty boxes and water and sand and playdough are so popular.

- **Eliminate or cut back on screen time.** Even having a television program or video playing as background noise can clutter a child's head and steal his focus.

- **Think before you buy.** Before adding new materials to your program, make sure you really need and have space for them.

- **Declutter your learning spaces.** Too much stuff can overwhelm kids and caregivers. Go through your environment and look for things you can remove. Uncluttered spaces offer more calm and help children focus.

Check out these books:

Last Child in the Woods: Saving Our Children from Nature-Deficit Disorder by Richard Louv

Taking Back Childhood: A Proven Roadmap for Raising Confident, Creative, Compassionate Kids by Nancy Carlsson-Paige

Consuming Kids: The Hostile Takeover of Childhood by Susan Linn

Free-Range Kids: Giving Our Children the Freedom We Had without Going Nuts with Worry by Lenore Skenazy

A Nation of Wimps: The High Cost of Invasive Parenting by Hara Estroff Marano

Zen Habits: Handbook for Life by Leo Babauta

From Jeff's World

Back in my high school days, I worked part-time in one of those big retail stores that sold everything from prescription medication to entertainment units. The downsides to the job were that I had to wear an orange smock to work, I got scolded if I forgot to take out my earring, and one of the managers kept riding me about my long hair. The upside was Christmastime. I loved the long lines and the commotion and making grouchy shoppers smile. While my coworkers dreaded this time of year, I thrived on it. This was in the prescanner days, when every price code was keyed in by hand—and I had fast fingers. I would clock in, sneak my earring back in as soon as I got to my register, and spend eight hours clicking away. I joked with the customers, speeding them through my checkout so they could head for the cold and slushy parking lot.

I didn't realize it at the time, but a big part of the joy I got from this poor-paying, mechanical job came from the feeling that I was doing Art. I brought a sense of play and fun with me to the job that many of my coworkers could not muster, so the long lines they focused on bogged them down, while I was having fun connecting with the people in those lines.

Next time you approach a checkout line, pay attention to the one you choose. Do you head for the one with the cashier who is upbeat and giving away free smiles, or do you head for the one with the cashier who looks like she would rather be anyplace than about to interact with you?

Now think about your interactions with children and how your mind-set influences how comfortable they are with you.

Value Vacation Mind-Sets

What if you approached your job with a vacation mind-set? What if everyone in your program did? You might find that your rulebook needed some changing. Teachers and administrators might relax a bit and go with the flow. Everyone might be less stressed. Honing a vacation mind-set is a great way to bring about thoughtful change to policies and procedures.

Think about your last vacation—not the time you spent packing and getting ready, not the time you spent traveling, not the time you spent getting back into the swing of your regular life once you got home—but the time you spent all settled in and relaxed at the beach or the campground or Grandma's house. Think about the mind-set you had during that time.

- You were not rushed.

- You were not stressed.

- You were free to play and enjoy yourself.

- You were unbound, unconfined, untethered, and unfettered.

- You were relaxed.

- You were invigorated.

- You were able to pursue interests for which you usually had no time.

- You were simultaneously able to engage and disengage.

- You were childlike in spirit and outlook.

- You were predisposed to *YES*.

- You were calm and centered.

- You were drawn to new ideas and adventures.

- You were able to let go and let your hair down.

- You were open to possibility.

A vacation mind-set is good for children as well, partly because they experience the same benefits of vacation that adults do, and partly because the adults responsible for them are more relaxed and less restrained. Kids are allowed more freedom to explore, dream, and play in vacation settings. It's easier to let them stay up late and chase lightning bugs with flashlights when no one has to get up early the next day. Here are some real-life examples of children freed up by the vacation mind-set:

A dark-haired, six-year-old girl wags her finger and scolds the Pacific Ocean every time it erases the lines she makes in the sand with the heel of her left foot. She repeatedly draws a fresh line in the sand, uses her fingers to urge the waves to come and get it, and then rebukes the water for doing what she's asked.

Sand-covered children take turns swinging each other too high in a rainbow-colored hammock. The swingee is cocooned in the cloth hammock as the swingers do their best to achieve a 360-degree rotation, a bit of danger outweighed by a lot of laughter.

Mud-encrusted campground kids catch buckets of toads by flashlight under a starry half-moon sky. Their shouts, roars, and giggles pierce the dark and push back its scariness.

Wellington-clad toddlers march down a rainy botanical garden trail, never missing a bug, stick, or puddle. Their noses are full of flowers, hands are full of treasures, mouths are full of questions.

An adventurous seven-year-old examines the moist wall at the dead end of a dark, 300-meter-long lava tube, trying to convince his mother to turn off her flashlight so he can "see what real dark looks like."

A nature-loving grandfather, time-polished Zippo in hand, explains to an increasingly curious grandson what it takes to make fire. The solid flick and instant flame of the trusty lighter pull the boy from his hand-held video game.

Five-year-olds dressed for the Fourth of July sell paper cups of lemonade for fifty cents, happily using their manners, practicing social skills with strangers, doing math, and mixing up yummy chemistry experiments with sugar, water, ice, and lemons.

A lone ten-year-old boy with long hair experiences wind in a grassy field. It tousles his hair, moves in waves through the long grass, shakes the trees, and makes his orange and green kite dance. It's all science, and it's all play.

If adults are less stressed and more relaxed and open on vacation, and if children are freer and more able to follow their own interests and whims, which we know builds brains, then why not hone a vacation mind-set all year long in your program?

Two reasons:

1. It's hard.

2. People just don't do that.

The first point is true. The second one is not.

Change is hard. If it were easy, then all the smokers who wanted to quit would be successful on their first try, everyone who wanted to lose and keep off weight would have washboard abs and upper arms that didn't sag like bread dough on a clothesline, and we'd all be living our dreams. Change takes time, energy, focus, and resources. It's scary, and you have to beat back the shadowy monster that fear creates in your head. On the other hand, people do hard things all the time. People do quit smoking. People do get in shape. People do live their dreams. Hard does not mean impossible.

As for the second point, some people *do* live with a vacation mind-set. Not just twentysomething surfer beach rats or seventysomething full-time campers pulling their fifth wheels from national park to national park all year long. Real people perfect mind-sets that let them live with the ease, focus, calm, and joy most people find only on vacation.

How can you change your mind-set from work to vacation? Here are a few tips:

- **Build a piece of every vacation into your everyday life.** Think about your last vacation and try to integrate something you loved from that time into your daily life. Maybe it will be taking morning walks as the sun comes up; listening to the birds sing in the evening; holding hands more with your sweetie; having a chance to read; connecting with your own children; or simply inhaling deep, clear breaths as you drift off to sleep. Making these vacation jewels part of your everyday life will keep you connected to your vacation mind-set, and you will feel the benefits.

- **Take baby steps.** Don't try to change too many things all at once or you'll just make a bigger mess. Look at the parts of your life that already support the vacation mind-set you're trying to create and make changes that magnify them. For example, if your Saturday morning routine is especially relaxing for you, try to build parts of that routine into your weekday mornings too.

- **Be your own troubleshooter.** Tune in to what makes the hard parts of your day so taxing and challenging and look for ways to reduce or avoid these stressors.

- **Make time every day to nurture your own needs.** Just a few minutes at the start of each day will do wonders. You will be more focused and mindful of the choices you make while caring for others if you make time to care for yourself.

- **See the joy that surrounds you.** It's there; you're probably just too busy to pay it any attention. When you see joy, take time to enjoy it and let it recharge you.

Changing your mind-set is hard, but you can do it if you choose to. It will lead to a happier life for you and a healthier early learning environment for the children in your care.

There are a lot of ways you can go about it. Start by stepping back from making quick decisions, and try to make thoughtful ones instead. Adults often find ourselves distracted by our hectic lives, personal stressors, and other obligations. Tuning in to the many day-to-day needs of children over the long haul can be daunting for parents, child care providers, teachers, and other caregivers. Taking time to make mindful choices is important for your own well-being as well as the well-being of the children in your care. The problem with mindfulness is that it takes a lot of time and energy and can be exhausting, but in the long run, it will even out many of life's ups and downs.

Continuity between your program's principles and policies and on-the-ground, day-to-day practices will make mindful decisions easier to make. Many programs are incredibly out of sync when it comes to these important pieces, and getting in tune would greatly benefit them—and the children in their care. Discordance between principles and practice can be very stressful. Consider changes you could make to bring your ideals and realities into alignment.

Cultivate coolness. We're not talking Fonzie-thumping-the-juke-box-at-Al's-Diner-and-making-a-Buddy-Holly-tune-play-while-two-cute-chicks-in-poodle-skirts-scurry-over-to-dance cool. We're talking relaxed cool: in-control-of-your-emotions cool, go-with-the-flow cool, nonjudgmental-it's-all-good cool. We're talking keep-your-cool cool, and cool-heads-prevail cool. Strong and healthy emotional environments for children require that adults don't run too hot. Kids have a hard time relaxing and settling in when they sense their caregiver is about to start sputtering, overheat, and belch steam everywhere. Kids need cool. Cool is comfortable.

Check out these books to help hone your mind-set:

Linchpin: Are You Indispensable? by Seth Godin

The Evolving Self: A Psychology for the Third Millennium by Mihaly Csikszentmihalyi

Seeking Balance in an Unbalanced World: A Teacher's Journey by Angela Schmidt Fishbaugh

Finding Your Smile Again: A Child Care Professional's Guide to Reducing Stress and Avoiding Burnout by Jeff A. Johnson

Keeping Your Smile: Caring for Children with Joy, Love, and Intention by Jeff A. Johnson

One more mindfulness tip: You have to have a Jenn.

From Denita's World

When it comes to maintaining a healthy mind-set, you have to have a Jenn. Jenns aren't available on craigslist or eBay. They're never in the

Sunday ad for Target or Toys"R"Us, yet they're a must-have for any early childhood professional or parent.

Are you following? Let me explain. A Jenn is a person you can bounce ideas off. A Jenn is someone you can call when you need advice or just a venting session. A Jenn is a person you can count on.

I was fortunate enough to meet my Jenn five years ago at the Family Child Care Professionals of South Dakota's annual conference. This first meeting was uneventful, holding only a few clues suggesting the amazing friendship that would evolve.

But it turned out Jenn and I had a lot of things in common. Among our many similarities is our shared passion for young children. We thrive on creating unique opportunities for young children, inspired by their interests, discoveries, and inquiries.

A valuable part of my friendship with Jenn is our ability to bounce ideas off each other. A fine example of this is a phone call I received from Jenn one day in May. "Denita! Quick! We're learning about the letter *R*, and I need something somewhat messy." Now, my brain can either be plumb empty or work very quickly, spewing out oodles of ideas. This day it came up with Rainbow Rain. I suggested to Jenn that she get the easels out, let the children paint, and then use water-filled spray bottles to squirt the wet paint and make it drip down the paper like rain. An hour later, Jenn called back to say, "Denita, thank you so much! You'll never believe what your idea turned into! We took the spray bottles outside, and the kids made their own rain. They had a blast just spraying the water, watching different objects change color and then wondering why others didn't change at all." Brilliant! An idea can quickly turn into another when two brains work together. (As for the Rainbow Rain, it turned into another fantastic idea: try it with washable markers instead of paint. Use markers to color across the top of the piece of paper, and then spray the washable color with water from the squirt bottle. The children love to watch the "rain" fall down their pages.)

Jenns are also valuable during those stressful moments of the day . . . those moments when you question the techniques you use to discipline or to help a child cope with her fear of bugs in a calm manner rather than screaming every time the ant sneezes. I think we can all relate to that challenge.

I know what you're thinking, and yes, Jenn and I talk on the phone while we're watching the children. Does this take away from the quality care we provide? Absolutely not. In fact, it raises the quality of care we provide, because we're meeting our own needs. We don't call simply to chatter about the latest blockbuster movie. We call to talk during those moments when we need a coworker, those times when we need to talk to someone who understands, and who understands *now*.

I think of the children who've been injured by an overstressed child care provider. If only that provider would have had a Jenn to call in that moment, a friend who understood and who reminded her that it's okay to walk away from the crying baby, as long as the little one is out of harm's way, a friend who said, "It's okay. You're only human. Stay on the phone with me until this moment has passed." You'll know when you've found your Jenn. Good places to look for

her are early childhood classes, conferences, and websites. If you work in a center or preschool, it's possible your Jenn is standing right in front of you.

Now that we've looked at practical ways to support an (un)curriculum, we're going to build on this foundation by examining ways to create engaging physical environment for children's play and discovery.

Creating Engaging Spaces

We have long viewed our imaginative life with a kind of sacred awe: as noble, pure, immaterial, and ethereal, cut off from our material brain. Now we cannot be so sure about where to draw the line between them. Everything your "immaterial" mind imagines leaves material traces. Each thought alters the physical state of your brain synapses at a microscopic level. Each time you imagine moving your fingers across the keys to play the piano, you alter the tendrils in your living brain.

—Norman Doidge, *The Brain That Changes Itself: Stories of Personal Triumph from the Frontiers of Brain Science*

Make no mistake about it, children are *always* learning: their busy brains are constantly making connections, sorting and classifying the world, and searching for understanding. Their curriculum is everywhere: their senses tingle, buzz, and crackle with input from the immediate environment. What they learn depends greatly on their physical surroundings.

Two-year-old Brenden excitedly places balloons in a box and delivers them to his caregiver. As he takes the balloons out of the box, he tells her the color of each one and expects her to hold them all at the same time, laughing with glee as her arms get fuller and fuller.

Four-year-old Katelyn dutifully circles *Mouse*, *Mountain*, and *Money* on a worksheet about the letter *M* while her longing and recently teary eyes dart across the room to the sensory table. After a trip to time-out, she has learned that her interests are not very important and that the teacher's interests are the ones that matter.

Daphne, one week after her three-month birthday, is reaching for soft blocks while older children build wooden block towers nearby. Daphne is coordinating her eyes and hands, beginning to master the mechanics of her body. She is also attuned to the sights and sounds of the older children's play.

Holding hands with his caregiver in the shade of a willow tree, Zack glares. He was caught climbing on the picnic table again. He yearns to challenge himself by pushing his limits and testing his skills, but he's been told repeatedly that climbing is dangerous. He has learned not to trust his body or his judgment.

Annie, four days before her third birthday, is reading *Blue Hat, Green Hat* by Sandra Boynton. She pauses to talk about the letters from people's names—"There's Siddha's *S*"; "There's Brenden's *B*." Annie is using the same inflection and tone in her voice that her caregiver does when she reads the book.

Creating an engaging physical environment is about more than the mere arrangement of furniture, toys, and materials. It is also about the *emotions* the environment evokes and the thoughts it engenders. Children experience their physical environments with all of their senses and their emotional selves. Brenden's excited balloon play and Daphne's first attempts at block play were moments of full engagement with the physicality of their environments. The flexibility of the empty cardboard box and the novelty of a mass of balloons to herd sparked Brenden to action. Daphne's explorations of blocks involved all her senses: tasting the block in her hand, feeling the vibrations of crashing towers in her ears and on her skin, watching the movements and faces of her playmates, smelling the fabric softener of the cloth blocks and the woodiness of the harder unit blocks. Annie's love of books grew stronger not only because of the presence of books but also because of the animation and joy she sensed in her caregiver's theatrical reading skills. Her caregiver's voice was such a part of Annie's environment that she incorporated its inflection and tone into her own reading. Katelyn and Zack learned from their physical environments too. They came away with what a lot of children take away from early learning programs: the idea that their interests are not a priority and that their judgments and assessments of situations are not valuable.

This chapter is not about your physical environment's square footage, staff-to-child ratio, number of degreed teachers in the room, quantity of multicultural toys on the shelves, number of learning centers, national accreditation status, or whether you have a posted daily schedule. These things can be important—and they get a lot of time and attention—but a preschool program with a lot of these can still be a physical space that represses play, discounts discovery, limits exploration, and hinders learning. These resources get talked about a lot in early learning because they're easy to document. It's easy to walk into a room and measure the activity space, count the number of kids and staff, review files, and look for a posted schedule.

To create a physical space that engages children and supports an (un)curriculum, caregivers need to look beyond easy-to-measure components and turn their attention to things that can be harder to quantify, things that can even seem counterintuitive. We hope this chapter will help you assess your physical space and the way it engages children in a new way.

To create physical spaces that support children as whole people who can manage their own learning, consider the ten principles that follow. Research shows that they promote healthy development and learning in children. Implement these principles and enjoy the engaging physical spaces full of opportunities for thoughtful learning that result.

- *Happy* BRAINS

- *Engaged* SENSES

- *Safe* DANGER

- *Abundant* TIME

- *Unbridled* CHITCHAT

- *Predictable* CHANGE

- *Thoughtful* STIMULATION

- *Appropriate* CHALLENGE

- *Real* WORK

- *Perpetual* MOTION

Happy BRAINS

In *Brain-Based Early Learning Activities,* Nikki Darling-Kuria writes, "The brain needs food, sleep, oxygen, water, and novelty and challenge to function" (2010, 11). Many early learning curriculums fail to attend to these research-based brain needs and end up pushing children in developmentally inappropriate and rigidly academic directions focused on teacher-centered activities, seat-work, and high-pressure testing. If early learning curriculums did consider the research, then kindergartners across the country would still get to take real naps during the school day, have a drink of water whenever they needed one, and have classrooms still full of dramatic play materials, playdough, blocks, and pet turtles.

If children's brains don't get what they need to function properly, learning and development can be limited. The human brain is not a hothouse orchid, but it does have some basic needs. Brains need a number of things:

- **Sleep.** Many brains do not get enough sleep for one reason or another. You probably know one, and you may have one.

- **Hydration.** Brains are mostly water, and they need enough of it to work their best, yet many programs limit or restrict the intake of liquids to cut down on trips to the bathroom or diaper changes.

- **Nutrition.** Healthy eating makes for healthy brains and bodies.

- **Oxygen.** This one seems easy, but environments with dust, mold, mildew, and other pollutants can affect health and then learning.

- **Exercise.** Brains need stimulation; that's what the *novelty* and *challenge* mentioned earlier are.

When you evaluate your own program, it's important to pay attention to your actual successes. See where you're already making choices that build happy brains. Do children get to sleep when they are tired and wake up on their own? Do you serve healthy meals, and do children eat them? Then look again to see what else you can do to build happier brains. For example, is it possible to make water available to kids whenever they want it? Keeping busy brains happy should be the primary goal of every early learning space. Any changes to your physical environment that help keep brains happy are well worth the effort.

To learn more about building happy brains, we recommend these books:

Nikki Darling-Kuria's *Brain-Based Early Learning Activities: Connecting Theory and Practice*

The works of Eric Jensen, currently master trainer and consultant to the Association of Brain-Based Learning in Education in Hong Kong: *Teaching with the Brain in Mind*, *Brain-Based Learning: The New Paradigm of Teaching* and *Arts with the Brain in Mind*.

Engaged SENSES

What sparks your memory? Do smells, sounds, tastes, and textures revive your past? For Denita, the scent of Love's Baby Soft perfume takes her right back to seventh grade. Certain tastes evoke cozy childhood memories, while others prompt horrible ones involving medicine. The texture of itchy lace brings back visions of an awful dress Denita wore in the seventies, while the soft, comforting feeling of velour reminds her of a pair of funky blue bell-bottoms she wore in kindergarten. Pictures of old farm tractors produce floods of memories of her farm-girl youth, and every time she hears the song "Footloose," she's instantly transported to the Crystal Theater in Flandreau, South Dakota.

This process works in reverse as well. If Denita thinks *Crystal The-ater*, "Footloose" pops to mind, while a memory of being sick draws out the odor of good old Vicks VapoRub.

All of which is more than just a nice little trip down Denita's memory lane. When our senses are engaged, connections are made. When you provide children with opportunities to learn, involve as many of their senses as possible. The more senses you're able to engage, the better. Stimulating the senses helps children remember, retain, and recall information as well as make new connections.

For example, if a child in your care shows interest in the letter *B* because it is his Buddy Bobby's Baby Brother's Birthday, you may want to create a learning opportunity for all of the children based on this inter-est, transforming your physical space into a celebration of all things *B*. You could offer bubble blowing, big blue balloon bopping, bears, bunnies, bubble wrap, bubblegum, blueberries, blue clothing, balancing, bouncing balls, baking banana bread, binoculars, beans, and blocks. You could also tape a giant letter *B* to the floor or trace and cut out *B*s so the children can glue buttons and other *B* things on them. Saturate your day with the letter *B* and focus on stimulating as many of the senses as possible.

This short list of *B*-related play inspired by a baby brother's birthday involves all the senses:

- Touching balloons, bubbles, bears, bunnies, blocks, bubble wrap, and bubblegum

- Smelling bubblegum, baking banana bread, blueberries, and beans

- Tasting bubblegum, banana bread, bubbles (hey, it happens), and beans

- Hearing bubble wrap popping, bopping blue balloons, tumbling blocks, and any bean-related noises

- Seeing blueberries, blue balloons, blue clothing, bubbles, and block towers

All these activities connect the letter *B* with rich sensory input, which in turn hardwires it into the children's busy brains. *B* then becomes much more than a squiggle on a piece of paper.

Because the senses feed the brain, it's important for caregivers to try to create engaging physical environments that appropriately stimulate children's senses. It's often easier to engage the senses of sight, sound, and touch, but the smell and taste should be captured, too, as should the sense of how our body is positioned in space (kinesthesia). For example, you could smell and taste things like bacon, blueberries, and broccoli and use your bodies to bounce, bend, and become the letter *B*.

Be aware that physical spaces for children frequently focus on the senses of sight and sound to the point of overstimulation. In your (un)curriculum, try to create spaces that take advantage of all the senses, but don't overemphasize any one of them. Simple and sensory-rich experiences like the ones outlined here stick in the brain, building strong memories, improving vocabulary, allowing children to better sort and classify their worlds, and providing a broader foundation for future learning. They also serve as a solid play-based foundation for later academic learning.

Here are a few tips for evaluating and enriching the sensory power of your program:

- **Solidify the value of sensory experiences in your own mind.** Think back to smells, textures, and tastes from your childhood. Jot down some memories of things that spring to mind—things like morning coffee brewing at Grandma's, the taste of paste in kindergarten, or the feel of a fluffy kitten.

_____

_____

_____

- **Get down to kid level.** Experience your physical space with all your senses. Then take notes about what you can do to build in more positive sensory experiences and neutralize any negative ones.

_____

_____

_____

- **Take a sensory inventory of your program.** Do children have opportunities to use all of their senses? If not, make an effort to make the environment more sensory friendly. Listen to your space: Do you hear a loud chaotic roar or a happy hum of engaged curiosity? How about smells? Does your place smell like a combination of bleach and Lysol? If so, consider doing a scent makeover to change your program's olfactory profile. Some home cooking or an open window can do a lot. Pay attention to how your environment affects your other senses too—and then make any appropriate changes.

_____

_____

_____

- **Play games.** Regularly provide children with new ways to stimulate their minds through their senses. Play games like What's That Smell? or What's That Sound? and introduce them to new materials they can explore with their senses. Make sure they have plenty of opportunities to use their senses to solve problems.

Safe DANGER

Everything is potentially dangerous. . . . *Everything.* Eating too much and eating too little are dangerous, stairs are dangerous, spending time in the sun is dangerous, spending too much time cooped up inside is dangerous. Go for a walk, and a branch could fall from a tree and kill you. Walk by a bowl of soup, and you could drown.

Caregivers should be concerned with the physical security and health of children. You need to take appropriate steps to assure that children are not exposed to excessive risk of injury or illness and maintain safe and healthy physical environments. That said, some programs and individual caregivers go to extremes that can actually hinder children's development in the name of safety.

Children need opportunities to experience safe danger so they can learn to manage risk. When it comes to managing risk, we need knowledge: the more we know about how the world works, the better we can understand which parts of it to watch out for. The problem with many early learning environments and with licensing standards is that they try to eliminate all risk, which gets in the way of children learning to effectively manage risks. Here are some examples:

- **Small bits and pieces can be choking hazards.** To eliminate risk, programs bring out their choke tubes or toilet paper tubes and get rid of everything small enough to fall through them. The problem? Not having tiny parts to manipulate slows small-muscle and sensory development.

- **Water play brings the risk of drowning and the spread of illness.** Many programs highly regulate water play or eliminate it entirely. Unfortunately, curtailing or eliminating water play steals a rich and healthy learning experience.

- **Many outdoor play spaces are made flat for the sake of safety.** If there are no hills or rugged surfaces, then little Owen is less likely to fall and scrape his knee. But without a few hills, slopes, or ruts, he also loses out on an opportunity to build large muscles, improve balance, and develop problem-solving skills. Changing elevations change a child's perspective. Being able to look down on the play yard or seeing the sand box from a slightly different angle, for example, helps children develop the orientation and mapping skills that are necessary for writing and math.

Experience plays a big role in learning to manage risk. Crossing the street alone for the first time requires looking for cars, being cautious, and moving mindfully. These skills can be acquired through practice with a responsible adult. But that is not enough. In the end, a child has to take the knowledge she has and step off the curb by herself, alone, for the first time.

Some readers probably gasped and clicked their tongues when they read about Brenden playing with balloons, since balloons—and tall metal slides, teeter-totters, hot dogs, and grapes—are now considered too dangerous for children. But here is why Brenden's balloon play was not dangerous: his caregivers made playing with balloons a safe danger. Brenden was in a group of six children and two vigilant, well-trained, experienced caregivers. He had experience playing with balloons, and if one broke, he knew what to do with the pieces. (Balloons just are not as dangerous as the media hype of the last few years has led people to believe. Back in the 1980s, eleven or so of the 63 million kids in the United States choked to death on balloons each year. These days that number has decreased to around six children per year out of about 74.5 million.)

Create physical environments that provide children with safe opportunities to play with danger. It's empowering for children to know that they're capable of facing dangers and things that are a bit scary. It instills confidence, builds autonomy, and improves self-regulation.

When it comes to health and safety, avoid the real dangers and downplay overblown fears. Instead, build opportunities for children to practice dealing with potential risks and dangers.

Here are some tips for bringing more safe danger into your program:

- **Read more on safe danger.** We recommend these books:

  Play: How It Shapes the Brain, Opens the Imagination, and Invigorates the Soul by Stuart Brown with Christopher Vaughan

  A Nation of Wimps: The High Cost of Invasive Parenting by Hara Estroff Marano

  Free-Range Kids: Giving Our Children the Freedom We Had without Going Nuts with Worry by Lenore Skenazy

- **Explore.** Investigate and explore your fears before banning items from your program.

- **Challenge.** Give children manageable problems to solve on their own, like "How can we get this big refrigerator box through the door and onto the playground?"

- **Create safe danger.** Come up with opportunities for children to test their limits in controlled environments. Try: "How high can you climb?" "Can you ride without training wheels?" "You go pick out some ice cream while I grab a loaf of bread."

- **Practice.** Provide children with the chance to practice being careful. This could mean hiking up a big hill or across some wobbly rocks; it could mean holding a live snake; it could mean slicing potatoes with a sharp knife.

Abundant TIME

The discovery of a bird's nest at Denita's resulted in over two weeks of learning. During that time, the children ate gummy worms as if they were birds, built nests that they would love to live in, dissected a bird's nest, and read story after story about birds. Finally, one day, just as quickly as birds had piqued their interest, the children made another discovery, and they were off on another adventure.

Giving children permission to exhaust an activity, game, story, song, or discovery honors their interests. It shows respect for their self-guided learning. Time is abundant; there should be no hurry, no rush—just time to savor moments to the fullest. Adults need to slow the rush of childhood and give kids more control over their time. Handing over control of time to children enhances the amount and depth of learning taking place in your physical environment. Kids will be happier and more engaged.

Kid Time and Adult Time are different. Adults can process information faster than children, and their thinking is more organized, so they can make sense of new situations and objects more quickly than kids. The world is a new place to children, and because their brains are busy developing, they aren't able to make decisions as quickly as adults. Children need time to process the world, to sort it out and classify it, which is why they are frequently distracted by bright and shiny objects and why simple tasks can take forever. They need time for repetition, time to categorize things, time to think, and time to explore—and they need time to eat. For example, at lunch Clint picks up a green bean and has it halfway to his mouth when a bumblebee banging against the window distracts him. Then the conversation between Samantha and Leroy grabs Clint's

attention for a few minutes before he watches Will's milk flow across the tabletop. Before you know it, fifteen minutes have ticked by, and that green bean still hasn't found its way into Clint's mouth.

Kids can move at a faster pace than adults. Sometimes in their rush to know the world, they move through an activity like an F5 tornado, leaving a trail of mayhem and destruction in their path. The thing is, whether children are moving quick as a cricket or slow as a sloth, their caregivers need to adjust programs to fit children's needs.

- **Be patient.** When you're patient, you take some of the pressure off kids, free them to explore some more, and strengthen the emotional environment. Growling at them to hurry up usually doesn't work too well anyway.

- **Operate on Kid Time.** Have a predictable schedule for important parts of the day, like meal and rest time, but don't let the clock control the day. Do your best to operate on Kid Time. Slow down and smell the playdough.

- **Let children exhaust opportunities.** Free children up to spend as much time on activities, projects, and interests as they desire.

- **Try to stay in the moment.** Your job is to give the kids what they need developmentally in the here and now, not to worry about they may need six months down the road. Besides, feeding children's current needs and interests is the best way to prepare them for the future.

Unbridled CHITCHAT

Engaging physical environments should be abuzz with chitchat. A room full of engaged children should hum with their talk. Writing and reading are important, but in the early years, conversation is king. The brain's focus is on building vocabulary, internalizing the rules of language, learning when to talk, when to pause and breathe, how to listen, how to put spaces between words, because whenyouruneverythingtogetherpeoplehaveahardtimeunderstandingyou.

A solid foundation of spoken language is an important step toward mastering reading and writing, yet too often caregivers try to do it all at once, even believing that it's beneficial to try to teach babies to read. Make use of the abundant time children have and talk to them—a lot. Make your program drip with rich language. Talk about everything you see, hear, do, touch, taste, and feel. Research shows that kids who hear the most language in their early years are the most successful students in school, and that hearing about fifty million words in their first five years is optimal (Bardige 2005).

Mealtime conversation is a prime occasion for language learning, but too often adults have a shut-up-and-eat mentality. They are often focused on getting through the meal as quickly as possible so they can clean up and move on to whatever is next on the schedule. Consider making mealtime talk-time, even if it takes little Clint over there at the end of the table forty-five minutes to finish his green beans because he has to tell the whole story about the real fire truck he saw going fast with its lights on and how his mommy had to pull over so it could go by and how then she started to drive again and then up the road they drove by the fire truck again but there was not a fire but one guy had a mask on and a thingy on his back. Remember, this is his childhood, and there is no need to rush him through it. Listen to his words. Ask questions. Engage in conversation. Explain that the thingy was a respirator that pumps fresh air into the mask so the firefighter can breathe. There is plenty of time to wipe down the table and sweep crumbs off the floor later.

Here are some more tips for encouraging unbridled chitchat:

- **Ask open-ended questions.** "What do you think?" "Tell me about your day." "How did you do that?"

- **Introduce new vocabulary often.** Give children a chance to experience new words. "See this string with the rock tied to the bottom hanging from the ceiling? It is a pendulum. Let's see what happens when we swing it."

- **Avoid saying, "No talking!"** If you ever catch yourself saying, "No talking!" to a group of children, step back for a moment and ask yourself, "Why?" Asking a child not to talk is like asking chocolate cake to stop being yummy or a baby spider monkey to stop being cute.

- **Dialogues trump monologues.** Hearing adults talk is helpful to children, but try to engage in *dialogue* with them rather than *monologue*. Talking *with* children is better than talking *at* children.

- **You don't have to have all the answers.** Remember that it's okay to say "I don't know" when a child asks you a question—and then add, "But I bet we can find out together" and do some research.

- **Books are important too.** Among other things, books start conversations, build vocabulary, and model language use. Have plenty of books in the environment, read them a lot, make sure kids of all ages have access to them at all times, and let kids see you reading. This shows them that it's a valuable skill used in the adult world.

Predictable CHANGE

Routines are valuable for helping children settle in and feel comfortable, but change is good too. Physical environments that never change become stagnant and boring. They become too predictable. Regular changes to children's physical environments keep things fresh and fire up their busy brains. Something as simple as placing the tote of Legos that usually sits on the table on the floor instead can shake things up and make the blocks seem new again. If baby dolls are usually only inside toys, the simple act of letting kids wrap the dolls in blankets and take them outside to play creates completely new play scenarios.

Regular, thoughtful changes not only stimulate learning but also influence behavior. A major cause of what's termed *misbehavior* in young children is boredom. Unique gets bored with the same old same old and starts thinking up new ways to challenge and stimulate her brain, which leads her to pull Zack's hair, pump all the liquid soap into the toilet, and see if the hamster can fly. Don't assume that Unique is a troublemaker with issues when out of the blue she starts tossing wooden blocks at her best friend's head. It may just mean that you need to spice up your block area a bit.

A few tips for making predictable change?

- **Rotate materials often.** Changing the available toys frequently keeps things interesting. If the stacking cups go away for a few weeks, they'll seem like new toys when you rotate them back into the classroom. Rotating learning stations or activity areas is good too. Nothing draws kids to the books or the blocks like having them go on vacation for a while.

- **Change the contents of your sensory table regularly.** Sand and dried rice are fun, but there are many more options out there. For example, try cracked corn, wood mulch, a mixture of baby oil and cornstarch, small stones, seashells, giant ice cubes, a sand and syrup mixture, or good old homemade mud.

- **Talk about change.** Encourage children to notice changes in and out of their classroom. Change your menus. They can become boring and predictable too.

- **Turn things inside and out.** Periodically put inside stuff outside and bring outside stuff in.

- **Toss some surprises into your day.** Nothing shakes things up like having a horse visit your playground, some piglets move in for a few days, or a surprise gallon of ice cream show up on a hot day.

Thoughtful STIMULATION

One of Denita's kiddos returned from a vacation to the ocean with beautiful photos to share and experiences to talk about. This child's experience generated lots of ocean interest, but Denita couldn't pack up her crew and take them to the ocean (it's a bit of a commute from South Dakota), and she certainly couldn't bring the ocean to them. Instead, she and the children read stories about ocean life, played with suction cups

When Play Vampires Strike

You've seen it before: Little Kimber, looking upset and lost, unable to engage with any of the materials or activities you've made available; Mica and KiKi having a hard time rekindling the marvelous baby animal hospital play scenario that had them so occupied before lunch; Baby Bubba staring off into space, even though he's surrounded by bright, beeping, buzzing toys. Children have a hard time finding, or reestablishing, play when Play Vampires strike.

Play Vampires are not the "I want to suck your blood" vampires or the "Vont to Buy My Chocolate Cereal" vampires or the "Oh, he's so dreamy and complicated and mysterious and dangerous and bad for me but I love him" vampires, or the "One banana ah-ah-ah . . . two bananas ah-ah-ah . . . three bananas ah-ah-ah. . . . Three! Three bananas!" vampires. Play Vampires don't rip your neck open for a drink of tasty blood, bark for a big breakfast-food conglomerate, seduce teen girls named Buffy or Bella, or hang out and randomly count things. Play Vampires suck play from children. Here are some common Play Vampires:

- **Physical discomfort:** A playful state of mind is not easy to find if you're thirsty, hungry, tired, or need to poop. Enough said.

- **Emotional discomfort:** Feelings of safety and security are vital. Children who do not feel emotionally at ease have a hard time relaxing enough to play. Emotional discomfort can come from ongoing situations in the child's home life or from little hiccups during their day, like a hurt feeling, a bumped forehead, or a tiff with a playmate.

- **Temperament:** A child's temperament may cause her to be slow to warm to new materials or changes in routine. The interplay of a group of children's temperaments—and their caregiver's—may also make play difficult. The group dynamic in a room full of preschoolers can compete with any television reality show or soap opera, and sometimes all of the hubbub can get in the way of play.

- **Overstimulation:** Young children, infants especially, can become overstimulated when their always-hungry senses are overfed. Babies will turn away from the stimulation and may even go to sleep to avoid the overload. For some children, too much sensory stimulation can hinder play as much as too little.

- **Time:** Our rushed schedules and hurried lives can get in the way of play. Too often caregivers chop a child's day into tiny blocks of time, and this can limit his creativity and play. It takes time to settle in, relax, build play scenarios, and find play.

- **No:** Some children hear the word *no* so often that they become uneasy trying new things and interacting with their environments. They're worried it will lead to another *no*.

Next time a child in your care has a hard time settling into a state of play, look for signs of a Play Vampire. If you discover that a Play Vampire is indeed the culprit, take steps to find a solution to the problem. (We feel compelled to warn you that wooden stakes are very rarely helpful solutions to a Play Vampire problem.)

similar to the suckers on an octopus's tentacles, put saltwater in the water table, and added materials to the learning space that inspired ocean-related play. Thoughtful stimulation brings experiences to young children that can open doors of curiosity, creating the desire to know more.

Sometimes caregivers aren't thoughtful about the quantity or quality of the stimulation they bring to their programs, leaving children either overwhelmed or underwhelmed. "Environments with too many predictable features tend to reduce the neural activity in the brain," writes Nikki Darling-Kuria in *Brain-Based Early Learning Activities: Connecting Theory and Practice.* "When the environment is challenging, a child's brain will continue to make new and more concrete connections. When we get used to certain patterns in our environment, we become less challenged" (2010, 33). On the other hand, too much unpredictability can have negative developmental effects. Physical environments that offer thoughtful stimulation more fully engage the busy and curious minds of young children and lead to more play-based learning.

Tips for creating opportunities for thoughtful stimulation:

- **Shun screen time.** Plenty of evidence shows that sitting in front of televisions and other screens hinders learning. Even a pile of empty cardboard boxes, scissors, and a few rolls of masking tape provide more interactive and developmentally appropriate ways to stimulate learning in young children.

- **Implement a battery-free zone.** Screen time is a big source of overstimulation, but there are others too. Consider all the electronic learning toys that whiz, whistle, and whirr. The sounds and flashing lights these gadgets make are sometimes the only interesting things about them. Kids get bored with them quickly, and the toys end up going unused. (Or the kids find creative but sometimes inappropriate ways to use them.) Avoid overstimulation by implementing a battery-free toy policy in your early learning environment.

- **Think about color.** Bright primary colors are not necessarily the most appropriate choice for walls and furnishings in an early learning program. Loud colors can overload the senses and influence behaviors. You are responsible for the whole feel of your physical space. Neutral walls with rich but subdued splashes of colors throughout the environment may provide stimulation that is more appropriate.

- **Think about clutter.** Do you have too much stuff in your space and on your walls? Does it ever change?

Appropriate CHALLENGE

Facing real challenges empowers children by testing their abilities, pushing their limits, and building their confidence. Facing real challenges is also invigorating. Imagine a child climbing an apple tree for the first time. Picture her tentative first steps as she finds her footing, and then the joy in her eyes as she moves higher and higher into the tree. Feel her heart pounding as she grasps limbs and manipulates her body, knowing that she is in total control of her situation.

The mind likes challenge. Physical environments should seek to offer children developmentally appropriate, personally interesting, and fresh challenges that build on prior knowledge. Challenges should engage curiosity, offer novelty, and include opportunities for failure and mistakes—when success is a predetermined outcome, challenges are not really challenges. Making mistakes and tasting failure are important experiences, and caregivers should help children embrace rather than avoid them. Ensure children have opportunities to engage with their physical environments in challenging ways.

Tips for creating appropriate challenges:

- **Create challenges for children to face together**. For example, when it's time to refill the sandbox, challenge a group of three- and four-year-olds to haul the sand from the driveway where the truck dumped it to the sandbox. This is real work, and the challenge of it will leave children flushed, excited, and empowered.

- **Create new challenges.** Learning happens when children are able to reach a bit farther than usual and see beyond their comfortable horizons. Help them see opportunities to push their limits and go a little beyond their comfort zone.

- **Use language that challenges.** Phrases like "I wonder if you can . . ." "What would happen if you . . ." and "Go ahead and try to . . ." can be incredibly motivating.

- **Praise children's efforts.** Facing a challenge is more important than completing it. Applaud the fact that the children tried. Your encouragement will empower them to try again and to learn from any mistakes they made during their first attempt.

Real WORK

Real work is good for children. It helps them learn responsibility, makes them feel like contributing members of their tribe, hones their skills, gives them a chance to practice solving problems, provides them with real-world challenges and problem-solving opportunities, builds their self-regulation and social skills, offers them firsthand, hands-on experiences, and empowers them. Plus, it feels darn good to look back at a job well done, even when you're only two, and all you did was carry a cantaloupe in from the car.

When you give children real work to do, ideally you will also give them permission to do it their own way, with just the right amount of adult support. This shows that you trust them, and it provides them with the opportunity to solve problems and to reason. It also feels good to be in control of the work and to have the autonomy to use their own judgment and knowledge. In his blog entry, "Whatever Happened to Labor?," Seth Godin (2010) writes, "We say we want insightful and brilliant teachers, but then we insist they do their labor precisely according to a manual invented by a committee." When you give children real work to do, give them support, but don't give them a manual on how to do it.

The work of play should offer real experiences too. Kids can spot phony, so adults should make every effort to offer them real-life experiences by doing the real thing. Instead of making a pretend campfire, build a fire; use real needles to sew; hammer real nails and saw real wood; play in real snow; offer opportunities to know the world with all the senses. When you're five and your heart is thumping as sweat beads your forehead on a chilly November afternoon because you just spent an hour and a half helping your caregiver stack firewood, the smile you smile when you look at the empty pickup bed and then at the neatly piled logs comes from a place deep inside you, and it warms you up.

You cannot turn the work of play into traditional adult-style work with all its pressure and deadlines and paperwork and Coglike requirements. "Forced education turns learning into work, something to be avoided unless there is an extrinsic incentive," Peter Gray writes in an e-mail message (January 18, 2010). Physical environments in which children can engage in real work, like tending tomato plants, fixing a broken table leg, or caring for a pet provide, valuable learning and life skills that are much more engaging and full of learning than staged activities.

Remember the following when you supply children with opportunities to do real work:

- **Have reasonable expectations.** The work you give children should be developmentally appropriate—at or just beyond their current ability.

- **Don't expect perfection.** One- and two-year-olds will be happy to help wipe the table after snack, but it's going to need an adult wipe when they are done.

- **Don't get tied into providing rewards for work.** Rewards devalue the process. Help kids understand that helping out is part of the social contract that goes into effect when you live with other people. There will be plenty of time to get paid for their help when they have mastered some skills.

- **Let children contribute.** When it becomes known that you value their help, children will find all kinds of ways to help you out. Give them the chance as much as practical and possible.

Perpetual MOTION

In *Brain Rules: 12 Principles for Surviving and Thriving at Work, Home, and School*, John Medina writes about how our powerful human brains developed while our ancestors were in motion. "Our fancy brains developed not while we were lounging around but while we were working out" (2008, 4). He explains that our hunter-gatherer ancestors were always on the move, covering up to twelve miles a day, and that the act of moving, along with the stimulation and sensory input we encountered, built our brains.

Now humans have become mostly sedentary, and the change affects our brains and bodies. The last thing adults should be doing is telling kids to sit down, keep their hands to themselves, and be quiet. The last thing adults should be doing is cutting recess and physical education and replacing them with more seat time. The last thing adults should be doing is telling young bodies built for motion, "Be still!" Medina writes, "Cutting off physical exercise—the very activity most likely to promote cognitive performance—to do better on a test score is like trying to gain weight by starving yourself" (2008, 24). How important does Medina think exercise is to thinking? He suggests replacing classroom desks with treadmills.

Children who are in motion are children who are learning. Physical environments that encourage motion are much more engaging and learning intensive than environments in which motion is curtailed. Children learn while they're in motion, so caregivers should make every effort to bring as much motion as possible into children's days. It's not hard to do, and there's no reason to buy a bunch of treadmills.

- **Stop standing in line**—or at least reduce line time as much as possible. Kids are not designed for standing in line, and it's boring to do.

- **Arrange your physical environment to promote motion.** Doing so is counter to what many programs practice. Caregivers are often in the habit of arranging furnishings to slow, limit, or stop children's movement.

- **Cut out (or reduce) screen time.** Screen time turns kids into drooling zombies. Turning off the screens leads to more movement.

- **Get outside and move.** A lot. Run. Go on long walks. Exhaust yourselves.

- **Move while you work.** When they prefer to be active, free children from mandatory sit-down rules during activities by letting them move around while they work. For example, there is rarely a reason why a child needs to stay in a chair during an art project. In fact, being forced to sit probably stifles her thinking. Real artists don't stay still—check out YouTube videos of Jackson Pollock painting. He is always in motion, approaching his work from different angles.

To make the most of playful learning, the spaces (un)curriculums offer children should be full of happy brains, engaged senses, safe danger, abundant time, unbridled chitchat, predictable change, thoughtful stimulation, appropriate challenge, real work, and perpetual motion. Once caregivers create such spaces, they can unleash children's interests and energy and let them lead their learning with the same passion and focus that Jackson Pollock brought to his canvases. But first caregivers have to trust the children. Read on to learn more.

Trusting Kids to Learn

People have often said to me, nervously or angrily, that if we let children learn what they want to know they will become narrow specialists, nutty experts in baseball batting averages and such trivia. . . . But healthy children, still curious and unafraid, do not learn this way. Their learning does not box them in; it leads them out into life in many directions. Each new thing they learn makes them aware of other new things to be learned.

> —John Holt, *How Children Learn*

The teacher's role is to be on the sidelines, offering support when needed to help children develop new skills and facilitating interplay between the child and the environment.

> —Nikki Darling-Kuria, author of *Brain-Based Early Learning Activities: Connecting Theory and Practice*, e-mail correspondence with the author (February 2010)

Babies may not have a whole lot of understanding about their world, but they know a whole lot about how to get it.

> —John Medina, *Brain Rules: 12 Principles for Surviving and Thriving at Work, Home, and School*

Letting a child lead scares a lot of people. It could mean elbow painting instead of fingerpainting; it could mean a stepladder in the block area to top off the tallest tower ever; and it could mean leeches in the water play table. Letting children lead could mean huge messes, utter chaos, and cotton candy for lunch. Trusting children to lead requires giving up some control, which can be discomforting and a tad bit daunting for caregivers used to controlling their program's curriculum.

Trusting children to lead their learning does not mean you abdicate your position as Adult in Charge. It does not mean sitting in the corner, reading *Cosmo*, doing your nails, and watching *Dr. Oz*—unless you want a *Lord of the Flies* scenario to unfold. Your job is vital to the process of children being able to lead their own learning, because while children are good at intuiting what they need to learn, they don't know much yet. They need you to shepherd them, support them, and have their backs when things get challenging or overwhelming.

Trusting kids means trusting play. It means empowering children, it means recognizing they understand what they need to know about the world, and it means seeing them as thinking and thoughtful individuals. Taking the leap of faith that trusting kids to guide their own learning requires means trusting in the innate power of play to hardwire brains.

The first step in trusting children to lead their own learning through play is to create a nurturing emotional environment. Only then can you move to the actual curriculum.

Emotional Environments

Here is an example of trusting kids to learn, shared by our family child care buddy Jennifer Henson.

> The kids were a bit curious when I moved our lunch tables aside, creating a big open space on the floor. I put a huge stack of newspapers down in the open space and sat down, and my audience grew. The children sat down beside me and watched as I opened one of the newspapers and looked at it. When I slowly ripped the newspaper down the middle, their eyes became wide with interest.
>
> Dylan grabbed a newspaper, as did Conner. They opened their papers, looked twice at me to make sure it was okay, and then laughed as they made their first tears.
>
> Being able to tear a newspaper takes practice, and it was fun to watch the younger ones bunch the papers together as they tried to

pull them apart. Then they watched their older friends making tears, and before long had it figured out too. Even nineteen-month-old Cole was giggling as he held a newspaper in his small hands.

In the process of tearing a newspaper apart, Emily noticed that the pages had letters and words on them. The older children then took turns finding the letters they knew, and they excitedly ran over to show me the letters. Ben, who loves cars, was ecstatic when he located the "cars for sale" section.

Before long, we had a huge pile of shredded paper. I realized we had a bit of a mess and probably were at a point where we should start to clean up. Suddenly, the children decided to throw great handfuls of paper up in the air, shouting "Newspaper rain! News-paper rain!" Paper was everywhere. My first inclination was to say "Stop!" but as the scene unfolded, I realized there was more learn-ing happening here than I could ever have imagined. The children weren't just throwing paper. They were seeing how high they could get it, how long it would take for the paper to fall, and predicting whether it would fall straight to the ground or bump into someone on the way down. The wonder and excitement on the children's faces made me realize that this was one of those moments when I just needed to sit back and see where the adventure would take us.

As it happens, our adventure took us to the "garbage dump" and the "recycling plant." The kids made trucks out of big tubs and loaded the papers into them, using plastic snow shovels. They even put on work gloves and hats for the big job. The recycling plant was all the way across the room, and the children had to push their loaded trucks over to it so the kids at the recycling plant could sepa-rate the garbage into piles.

This adventure was completely unplanned, driven entirely by my little friends. We made many memories, had lots of laughs, and learned a whole bunch in the process. Without even realizing it, the kids practiced their fine- and gross-motor skills, their teamwork skills, their math and science skills, and their language and literacy skills. And to think that it all came from a big stack of newspapers!

Set the stage to make moments like this happen in your child care programs and homes. Kids need the freedom to explore and imagine at their own pace and in their own ways. Remember that the simplest objects produce the most amazing experiences. Don't be afraid of a little mess, or you'll miss out on some really fun experiences. At the end of our particular adventure, the children had all of the papers loaded in a garbage bag for the real garbage man to haul away the next day.

Jenn's success letting children lead stems from the strong emotional environment she's been able to create in her program. Swiss psychologist Jean Piaget long ago recognized children's need for healthy social relationships in order to grow into capable adults, but in recent decades the push to rush children into academics has overshadowed the value of positive relationships in many early learning programs. "Overemphasizing the development of what's between the ears can wind up deemphasizing the development of what needs to be in the heart in order to foster happy, confident children who can cope with the disappointments and roadblocks life invariably metes out," write Kathy Hirsh-Pasek and Roberta Michnick Golinkoff in *Einstein Never Used Flash Cards: How Our Children Really Learn—and Why They Need to Play More and Memorize Less* (2003, 200–201). This is a problem.

Healthy emotional environments not only create a comfortable zone for play-based learning to take place; they also prepare children for the emotional thrill ride they will experience throughout life. Remember little Gabby from way back in chapter 1? The transition from an environment in which she felt safe, comfortable, and loved to a new one in which she had no roots caused her a great deal of stress. Humans are social creatures; we need positive connections with the people around us to thrive. Piaget and other observers and thinkers have asserted this belief, and modern neuroscience has confirmed that the brain learns best when it is socially at ease in a trusting environment. All busy young brains deserve emotional environments that instill feelings of comfort, calm, and connection.

Caregivers should strive to create emotional environments that offer emotional security and safety, instill a sense of belonging, and nurture individuals. Does your program's emotional environment feel calm and relaxed or stressed and tense? It matters.

Parents and professional caregivers we questioned for this book told us stories of their first few years of child care and formal schooling. As you read through their comments below, try to imagine the emotional environments their memories might have sprung from.

"Mrs. Crump was my first grade teacher, and we loved her, lining up to hug her as we left for the day."

"I loved school. It was a happy place for me."

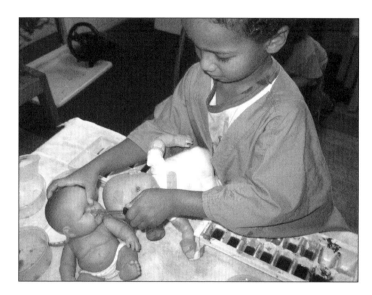

"I was horrified to learn that my imagination wasn't celebrated [at school] as it was at home."

"I was very shy and a rule follower. I was afraid of my teachers."

"I was shy and had anxiety over new classrooms, teachers, and peers."

"I went to public school and in first grade witnessed a student getting hit with a yardstick because she couldn't do a math problem. I also recall an incident in third grade where the teacher would not let a student go to the restroom and the poor girl wet herself at her desk and cried for the rest of the day. My kindergarten teacher, however, was wonderful. She used play-based learning, humor, and lots of love."

"Miss Ewart was so strict, and I was scared of her and most of the other teachers. They were big people (tall) and made some children cry a lot of the time."

"In third grade I remember being yelled at every day by the teacher, Miss Reineer, for not understanding math. I still panic now!"

"I remember getting in trouble in kindergarten because I cut outside of the lines. I was not good with scissors. I remember being embarrassed a lot. I was a very shy child."

Many of these experiences touched on the difficulty of making transitions and feelings of being lost, alone, and powerless. We heard a lot of tales about authority figures who habitually belittled students—or worse. Some commented on the lasting influence that one bad experience with an adult caregiver in early school years had on their view of a subject— mathematics, handwriting, gym—to the point that it still haunts them to this day.

We heard about positive experiences too: teachers who were loved so much that kids stood in line for hugs, teachers' humor, and how school was a happy place. The emotional memories we carry away from our learning experiences stick with us for a long time and influence who we turn into as adults.

These memories, from adults in the United States, Ireland, England, and Australia, show the importance of the emotional environments that caregivers create for children and how memories of emotional spaces can stay with children for decades to come. Yet many programs pay more attention to physical than to emotional space: the carpet is vacuumed, the toilets are cleaned, and the changing table is disinfected, but the emotional landscape is not given due attention. Programs often fail to attend carefully to the emotional needs of the people occupying their physical space. Caregivers' stress and frustration are glossed over by administrators—"I know the two-year-olds are a handful, but it's just part of the job"—in hopes that they will go away. Children's outbursts are downplayed—"Be a big boy and stop your crying"—because understanding the emotional causes at their core can be difficult and time consuming. Relationships with parents are kept shallow because deepening them requires additional emotional labor. For the well-being of children, it is imperative that caregivers take a thoughtful approach to the day-to-day feel of their programs.

We're going to look at five concrete ways to build a healthy emotional environment for your early learning program that make it easier to trust children as they lead their own learning:

- Clear your mind.

- Deal with it.

- Be solution focused.

- Adjust your stories.

- Remember, you're a model.

CLEAR YOUR MIND

Remember Jeff's teacher, Miss Rogers? It's very likely she was not the fire-breathing, evil hag he remembers. Maybe what he saw in her as mean and scary was really stress, frustration, or burnout. Maybe she had other things on her mind. The real world often clouds adult focus, getting in the way of creating strong emotional environments for children. It's hard to focus on Hot Wheels cars flying off the racetrack and smashing a block tower when you argued about toast with your sweetie fifteen minutes before leaving for work.

Let's face it: real life can be messy, and it's not always easy to exclude it from the classroom. Children thrive in the care of focused caregivers who are able to offer respectful care in the moment, but none can be that person all the time. Over the last few years, Jeff has compiled a list of things that caregivers in his stress and burnout trainings identified as distracting them from focusing on emotional environments. Here are some of them:

- "Lack of preparation time"

- "Poor pay"

- "We don't get breaks."

- "My temperament sometimes is in conflict with some of the kids."

- "I can't seem to leave my personal emotional baggage at home."

- "Constant cleanup takes too much of my time."

- "Our director is burning out, and it affects the whole staff."

- "My agency lost funding, and it looks like we are going to have to close."

- "My job is not fun anymore, but I don't have any other options."

- "There is lots of pressure from parents and supervisors to 'Teach' instead of letting kids play."

- "Lack of personal understanding/knowledge about the process of play-based learning"

- "Multiage groups"

- "Homogeneous groups"

- "I'm afraid of doing it wrong."

- "Working with the wrong age group"

- "The cancer is back."

- "My feet hurt."

- "Relinquishing control"

- "Methmommies"

- "Paperwork gets more of my time than the kids do."

As you can see, there are plenty of ways clouded minds can interfere with emotional environment. The human mind thinks, and at times that thinking weighs heavily.

Here are some tips for clearing your busy mind so you can be more in the moment:

- **Make time every day to meet your own needs.** You will be in a much healthier state of mind if you devote some of your precious time to following your dreams, managing your mind-set, and actively pursuing your goals. Caregivers often get so busy attending to the needs of others that they place their own physical and emotional well-being on the back burner. They think they don't have time for self-care, or they're not worthy of it. This sort of thinking can launch a downward spiral that ends in burnout. Making time for you own needs makes you better at meeting the needs of others.

- **Every now and then, make a quick stress list.** Take five minutes and a piece of paper and list the things that are stressing you out, cluttering your thinking, and stealing your focus. This simple act can drain the clutter and chaos from your head and allow you to be present.

- **When you start feeling overwhelmed, take a few long, deep breaths.** This creates a space between you and whatever it is that's straining your mind-set.

DEAL WITH IT

Unfortunately, you can't just clear your mind and expect everything to be better. A few long breaths may help you set aside the anger and frustration you feel about the speeding ticket you got on the way to work, but you still have to deal with the ticket—and the anger and frustration. You can empty the turmoil from your head and improve your attitude and outlook for a while, but if you don't deal with it in a deeper way, all that clutter will come back eventually.

Clearing your head works only for the short term. If you don't deal with the things that are bothering you, they're going to seep into your dreams, keep you from sleeping, and become harder and harder to simply set aside. Here are some tips you can use to deal with problems.

- **Make time every day to work on the things in your life that need work.** Even as few as ten or fifteen minutes of focused attention every day can help you work through the things that are clouding your mind—and have a huge impact on your emotional environment. The things that weigh on you won't weigh as heavily when you feel as if you're making progress in dealing with them.

Communications

Free, open, honest, and respectful communication is another hallmark of a program with a healthy emotional environment. Sadly, it's sometimes the case that caregivers working in the same room can barely tolerate each other or speak civilly; communication with parents is abrupt, disrespectful, and belittling; and directors rule with the ferocity of Genghis Khan. While these situations are atypical, most programs could upgrade the way they communicate. Effective communication sharpens and deepens relationships, builds and demonstrates mutual respect, and instills and increases personal confidence—it strengthens emotional relationships. If the adults involved in an early learning program can't talk nice and work together effectively, then the program's emotional environment suffers.

Pay attention to how your program's handbook and other printed documents communicate.

Do you do what your brochure says you do? Do your promotional documents, staff policy books, website, and the building you work in reflect an open and engaging emotional space? Consider what the language and dress of staff members might be communicating; do they look and talk like they're ready to support the work of play? How do the staff, parents, and children who have left your program communicate about it? Did you provide them with an emotional environment that they praise to others, or do they have negative things to say?

Take time to evaluate your program's spectrum of communication, and then accentuate the things you do well and work on a few of the things that need improvement. When you do, you're taking a step toward a healthier and more inviting emotional environment.

- **Dealing with some things that keep you from being in the moment may require a shift in thinking**. For example, the Big Hurt from your childhood that still gets in the way of your adult relationships may need to be reframed from something that defines you to something that is simply a part of your past. It isn't easy to shift your thinking, but when you do, you take away the power the darker parts of your life have over your present interactions with the world.

BE SOLUTION FOCUSED

Our society is acutely focused on problems both real and imagined. The news and other media thrive on pointing out, magnifying, exploiting, and even creating problems. We're told to prepare for the worst; after all, no one ever says as you head out the door, "Hope you're prepared for the best! You never know what unexpected and wonderful thing could happen!" Naming, sharing, and focusing on problems comes naturally and easily to most of us.

We hold both nature and nurture responsible. Early in our human history, being able to see potential problems was important because we were exposed to things that wanted to eat us. Evolution wired our brains to pay special attention to signals indicating impending danger and approaching problems. We paid attention and gave our focus over to the dark clouds on the horizon, the rustle of tall grass on a breezeless morning, or the brackish, stagnant smell of a just-discovered watering hole. Seeing problems quickly often meant the difference between life and death.

Nowadays, most of us spend little time worrying about thunderstorms, saber-toothed tigers, or bad water, but it's still in our nature to pay attention to potential problems. Heck, we're wired to do more than pay attention to them—we're wired to focus on them over everything else.

This wiring influenced how we were nurtured as little ones. Most of us grew up in settings in which problems were given more attention than nonproblems. Flaws were pointed out and accentuated more than successes, bad grades were discussed more than good ones, and bad behavior grabbed more headlines than good behavior.

Problem-focused mind-sets are incredibly common, and while they can protect us from certain dangers, they can often get in the way of child-led learning. For example, when many adults hear the words "mud play," their minds jump straight to messy clothing that will need changing, dirty hands and toes that will need cleaning, and sloppy handprints on white walls that will need scrubbing. It's harder for many to see that mud play also means the development of small and large muscles, hand-eye coordination, problem-solving skills, sensory awareness, creativity, spatial relations and geometric thinking skills, preliteracy and prenumeracy skills, and a sense of fun and adventure. Adults tend to see the problems something like mud play will cause with sharper focus than they can see the good mudplay can do the children in their care.

We need to shift from a problem-focused mind-set to a solution-focused mind-set. Problems will still come up and need to be dealt with, but a shift in mind-set will help open us up to solutions.

In Milwaukee, Wisconsin, back in the late seventies, Steve de Shazer, Insoo Kim Berg, and their colleagues developed a new type of brief therapy now known as Solution-Focused Brief Therapy, or SFBT. Traditional therapy often takes years and involves lots of time talking about problems and their causes. Solution-Focused Brief Therapy doesn't pay attention to the past. It focuses on the present and future. In fact, it focuses not on just any future, but on the client's *preferred future*—the future the client would like to create for himself. It looks at the client's current successes in life as well as at ways to accentuate and expand on those successes in order to bring about the client's preferred future. As a professional caregiver, you can take advantage of some SFBT concepts to help shift your mind-set and become more solution-focused in your day-to-day life. It takes effort to see solutions if you're accustomed to seeing only problems.

Here are some steps you can take to shift your mind-set and start seeing solutions:

Jot down a paragraph or two describing your preferred future.

_____

_____

_____

_____

_____

_____

_____

Reflect on the things that are going well in your life right now and then try to build on those successes.

Pay attention to your thinking by periodically asking yourself if you're being problem focused or solution focused.

Check out these books:

> *More Than Miracles: The State of the Art of Solution-Focused Brief Therapy* by Steve de Shazer and Yvonne Dolan

> *Keys to Solution in Brief Therapy* by Steve de Shazer

ADJUST YOUR STORIES

Paying attention to the stories we tell ourselves and others can serve as a barometer of our emotional environments. Our stories can inspire or hinder. Our stories can influence our actions and attitudes. Changing our stories can change our outlook.

Listen to the stories that play in your head as you go about your day, and pay attention to the words that leave your mouth when you tell stories about your work to others. If your stories are full of stress, frustration, and anger, then the emotional environment you've created is probably not as healthy as it would be if your stories were full of smiles, hope, and success. Adjusting your stories can help mend your outlook, and doing so will strengthen the emotional environments you create.

For example, shifting your story from an "I'm a babysitter, my job is drudgery, I just watch kids" story to an "I'm an Artist, my job is valuable, I wire brains for a living" story can have a big impact on how you relate to children during the course of the day. It can also work in specific situations or with specific children: shifting from a "Kimmy is a wild child" story to an "I love Kimmy's energy" story will change the way you respond to little Kimmy the next time she makes a pair of construction paper wings and tries to fly off the activity table.

Here are some suggestions for adjusting the stories you tell:

- **Read *The Story Factor: Inspiration, Influence, and Persuasion through the Art of Storytelling* by Annette Simmons.** It's a fun read about the power of stories and how to use them better as teaching tools.

- **Pay attention to the way you talk when things are going right.** Focus on the language you use in talking about your beliefs, values, and strengths when your emotional environment is healthy. Then, when things go sideways, try to build that healthy language into the stories you're telling. Changing just a few words can change your outlook: "My mind is cluttered today. I'm going to explode!" can become "My mind is full of ideas today. I'm going to write them down."

- **Pay attention to the stories you tell when you face turbulence.** Make sure to step back and look at the stories you're telling about the turbulent situation, and then look for ways to adjust the stories so you can approach the situation from a different perspective. For example, if the story you tell yourself about rough-and-tumble play is that it's too dangerous and aggressive, consider changing that story to one that depicts rough-and-tumble play as an opportunity to build large-muscle skills, practice social skills, and develop self-regulation skills. This shift in your story can turn panic caused by a herd of rambunctious kids stuck inside on a rainy day into a learning-filled morning of mud wrestling in the rain.

REMEMBER, YOU'RE A MODEL

All of us have bad days. Nonetheless, adults who work with children are always modeling for children. Are you modeling the behavior you want to see from children? The truth is, children are always watching you and learn a great deal more from your actions than from your words. Just keeping in mind the idea that you're a professional role model can influence your emotional environment. What do your actions and attitudes say to children? Do your actions match your words? Consider the following:

- Do you say what you mean?

- Do *you* use language effectively to manage your emotional environment?

- Do *you* use your manners?

- Do *you* share and take turns?

- How do you manage frustration, disappointment, or anger?

- Are *you* being the kind of person you want the children to become?

Children are incredibly intuitive. Their mirror neurons allow them to tune in and experience the emotional state of the people around them, yet caregivers often fail to pay attention to the emotional environments they're creating. Not paying attention to the emotional state of your program affects children's learning. Fortunately, with some mindfulness and effort, you can create a program that is physically and emotionally inviting, engaging, and nurturing.

Play-Deprived Children

Play is innate, but some children grow up in situations in which they aren't exposed to a culture of play, exploration, and discovery. They come to you without a culture of literacy, a culture of problem solving, or a culture of dependable adults. Some kids spend their earliest years in situations in which they have little contact with other children, books, or the toys most of us take for granted—blocks, baby dolls, crayons, playdough. Some come to you closed off and withdrawn, the effects of their stormy pasts.

These play-deprived children need your special attention. They need you to help them learn to embrace play, face challenges, and cuddle up to literacy. Working with play-deprived children takes effort and perseverance. Acclimate them to the culture of play and give them opportunities to lead their own learning. You may need to use materials and activities typically reserved for much younger children so the foundation they missed building in their younger days can be built. Don't push them into academics, drills, or seat work to make up for lost learning.

Luckily, the human brain is incredibly resilient and the windows of learning never shut completely. This means that with time, attention, and effort, play-deprived children can get on track and eventually lead their own learning. The second edition of *Beyond Behavior Management: The Six Life Skills Children Need to Thrive in Today's World* by Jenna Bilmes is a good resource to check out.

Trusting Children

Once you've built a solid emotional environment, you can begin to look for ways to trust children and allow them to lead their learning.

Here are nine research-supported suggestions to help you trust children to lead their own learning. Think of them as tools for your (un)curriculum toolbox.

- Allow leeway.
- Keep it real.
- Value process over product.
- Make *yes* easy.
- Support with words.
- Back off a bit.
- Nudge when needed.

- Embrace mistakes.

- Avoid awards and praise.

ALLOW LEEWAY

Remember Daniel Pink's four Ts —Tasks, Time, Techniques, and Team? When you give children control over the four Ts, you provide them with a huge amount of leeway—*and* control over their learning. Leeway gives children control over their learning, and being flexible and letting kids set their own agendas frees them up to learn the things they're primed to learn. Winston Churchill said, "Personally, I'm always ready to learn, although I don't always like being taught." Most people feel this way—children included. The four Ts give kids leeway—the freedom to explore and discover the world. They also give them power and control over their learning.

In an (un)curriculum, his adult caregiver gives three-year-old Keith control over the four Ts when Keith shows interest in the way wind blows dandelion puffs across the playground. Keith gets to make "know more about wind" his task. As his exploration of the topic unfolds, Keith may decide to give it ten minutes of his time, or he may decide to devote hours to the topic—either way, Keith gets to decide. When it comes to techniques, Keith is given a lot of freedom. He may decide to blow every dandelion puff he can get his hands on. He may decide to start tossing handfuls of grass or shredded paper or leaves or sand into the air to see how they move in the breeze. He may decide to plop down on his back and watch the wind dance in the trees. He may decide to draw or paint the wind. The caregiver's job is to be supportive, provide materials, and offer just enough support. Keith may want to work alone—or he may decide to pull together a "Know More about Wind" team to help him in his play-based exploration. In an (un)curriculum, the decision is his to make.

While allowing children leeway in their play can stir up a bit of fear in adults who are used to being in control, caregivers must remember that children can and should be the leaders of their own learning expeditions—caregivers are simply the trusted and knowledgeable Sherpa guides. Caregivers assist, support, and suggest, but children should be in charge of the journey. This leeway helps them learn to lead, make decisions, and learn from mistakes.

Patricia Murray, former president of the International Family Day Care Organisation and Chief Executive of the National Childminding Association of Ireland, told us she had a lot of leeway in her childhood play. Her favorite play activity as a young child was constructing hideouts, which gave her and her playmates the chance to assert "independence from adults by creating our own secret spaces" and to learn "construction, resourcefulness, to plan, to modify, to use whatever came to hand to build dens, tree houses, wigwams, and even Wendy-houses." (If you've never heard the term, a *Wendy-house* is a small playhouse named after the structure the lost boys in *Peter Pan* built around Wendy when she was injured shortly after her arrival in Neverland.) Patricia and her playmates were able to build these secret spaces free from adult intrusion and oversight.

Patricia told us this story too:

> With my sister and two pals, following the discovery that water could change colour by adding various materials, we gathered every possible container—glass bottles and jam pots—everything was glass then, before the plastic era—and we made fifty-seven different coloured jars of water using coloured dissolved sweets, ink, berries, anything that made a colour! We were at it for two or three days during the summer holidays. We lined them up against the white wall of the house in the sunlight, and were so proud! Mum, bless her, left them there long after we'd lost interest, but disposed of them before they grew green mould!

Control over the four Ts and the leeway that came with it created a great self-directed learning experience. Patricia said, "We planned, we scavenged, we measured, we poured, we counted, we explored, we experimented, we argued, we cooperated"—and they did it all without a well-meaning adult hovering over them.

From our buddy Jenn comes another example of the fun and learning that allowing children leeway can provide:

> Flyswatter painting—that's what I thought we'd try. Armed with a roll of paper, paint, flyswatters, paper towels, and a bucket of water with soap, we headed outdoors. But as I unrolled the paper and squirted

the paint on plates, all of the children abandoned me and headed back into the garage and decided to get the bikes out.

Did I call them all over and ask them to paint? No. I decided to wait and see what would happen. After some time, the first child walked over, put a flyswatter in the paint, hit it on the paper, and walked away. I watched him go and wondered, "Will anyone want to paint today?"

After a while, Dylan and Emily walked over and gave it a try. When they were done, they put their flyswatters in the bucket of soapy water to wash them off. Never would I have guessed it, but from that simple act, the real fun began! The kids swirled flyswatters in the soapy bucket a couple times and noticed that the water was changing. It wasn't just water anymore; it had bubbles in it too! The kids laughed as the bubbly suds got bigger and bigger, and they told me they were making soup. Before long, all of the children had abandoned the bikes and joined in.

Next came another surprise: the soup became snow flying in the air and pancakes flipped onto the driveway. Then Emily noticed the roll of paper towels lying in the grass and asked if she could have a sheet. She dipped it into the bucket of soapy water and squeezed it out. The water slowly spread across the ground and began creeping down the driveway. Fascinated, everyone decided they needed a paper towel, and soon I had tons of little rivers running down my driveway. Over and over the children repeated this process until Conner took a flyswatter and splatted one of the rivers. The water fanned out, and the amazement on his face was apparent. The children ran out to splat the rivers before the water could reach the end of the driveway.

Next the fun moved from down on the ground in the driveway into the air. The children used the flyswatters as launchers, and soon wet paper towels were flying through the air like planes. Again and again the kids watched as the paper towel airplanes flew up and crashed down. The children noticed that when the planes hit the ground, they flattened out on the pavement. When they picked up the wreckage with their fingers, it would change shape again, becoming snakes, ropes, and worms. Soon all the kids had paper towel sculptures to share.

I was amazed: forty-five minutes had gone by! Would flyswatter painting have engaged the children for that amount of time? Probably not, but what had happened instead was so much better. Never would I have guessed that a bucket with squirts of soap in it, flyswatters, and a roll of paper towels could provoke so much learning and be a source of so much fun! It's wonderful the way everyday objects the children may or may not be familiar with can inspire so much play and learning.

Tips for providing children more leeway:

- **Look at your own life.** How do you feel when you're capable of doing something on your own and then someone pops in with unsolicited advice about how to do it better, faster, more efficiently, or "right"? It kind of sucks out your inner drive, feels belittling, and steals a bit of your personal power, doesn't it? Kids feel the same.

- **Limit rules.** Adult rules are often enforced arbitrarily and can get in the way of learning. For example, the "use little drops of glue" rule gets in the way of the child's developmental need to squeeze (which builds strength in wrists and supports writing); the "don't waste paper" rule makes no sense to a three-year-old artist wrapped up in the creation process; and the "keep your hands to yourself" rule flies in the face of a child's biological need to connect physically with peers. These kinds of rules are intrusive and impossible to enforce, and they hinder development. If you need rules, let the children have a hand in making and enforcing them.

- **Encourage adult-out play**. Early learning is about children's learning, not about adults' teaching. Adult-out play happens when adults fade into the background and is extremely important for young children. It allows them opportunities to problem solve, be creative, and explore their world without the influence of preconceived adult ideas. Adult minds know boundaries and limits. Adult minds assign particular functions to certain objects: a door is a door, and that is what it shall always be. Adults can have a hard time stepping outside the boundaries . . . coloring outside the lines. Adults' lines are typically drawn in permanent ink, while children's lines are made of sand—lines that can be easily shifted and changed to meet particular needs. Adult-out does not mean you get to go AWOL. It means you become stage manager.

- **Make *yes* easy.** *No* is intrusive.

- **Allow children as much power and control as they can developmentally manage.** Managing power and control takes practice, so give kids just enough to get the practice they need. Giving three-year-olds free access to the scissors and glue once they've shown they can behave responsibly with them and allowing two-year-olds to carry their own plates to the table at mealtime are examples of this.

KEEP IT REAL

We humans all learn better from real-life experiences than we do from staged learning. If you're two and someone tells you, "The stove is hot. Don't touch it!" then you haven't really learned anything. You've been given useful information, but because you haven't experienced a hot stove, the wiring for "Don't touch the stove!" isn't very strong. If, however, you go ahead and touch the hot stove, you immediately understand "Don't touch the stove!" Touching the hot stove once is enough to keep many of us from wanting to do it again, but others among us require a few more touches before "Don't touch the stove!" is hardwired into our brains.

Let's think about chocolate cake. Did you learn about chocolate cake from reading about it, hearing someone talk about it, seeing pictures of it, watching a video about it, studying a recipe for it, or eating a hunk of angel food cake? No, you learned about chocolate cake by experiencing a hunk of real chocolate cake. You had an experience that involved all your senses: the sweet smell, the texture on your tongue, the sound of your own chewing or maybe of "Happy Birthday," the sight of the thick frosting, and the rich, yummy taste. *Real*, authentic experiences that we feel with our whole selves are the ones that stick with us and hardwire our brains. When it comes to brain development, a simulated experience is not an alternative to the real thing.

Trusting kids to lead their own learning requires that caregivers make a wide and deep variety of real experiences available to them. *Real* learning opportunities literally surround the children in your care.

Everything they're able to interact with is a chance for *real* learning: the bag of oranges on the kitchen counter, the bird's nest outside the classroom window, UPS Guy waiting for a signature, the emptied box and the bubble wrap inside the package delivered by UPS Guy, the muddy puddle in the driveway, the apple tree on the playground. A caregiver's job is to provide experience, not to decide what kids are going to learn, and while caregivers can anticipate some of the learning outcomes, each child will come away with her own learning based on her own personal experience.

The problem is that adults often stage experiences that imitate *real*— and these staged experiences tend to be less engaging, less meaningful, and less fulfilling than the *real* thing. Think about your own life. Do you enjoy *staged* experiences and activities as much as those that feel *real*? Cutting playdough with a plastic knife is not the same as cutting an onion with a real knife. Hammering a golf tee into a hunk of floral foam is not the same as hammering a nail into a piece of wood. Catching a laminated cardboard fish with a clothespin is not the same as reeling in a real fish. *Real* activities come with *real* exertions, *real* smells, *real* effort, *real* textures, *real* engagement, *real* complexity, and *real* dangers that the staged activities cannot replicate.

Boxed Curriculums

When we reviewed some boxed curriculums in preparation for writing this book, we came across a great many staged activities that to us felt contrived, phony, and gimmicky. In many of the cases, 95 percent of the hands-on, active parts of the projects were supposed to be done as prep work by the adult. In an (un)curriculum, if an activity requires cutting, the scissors should be in the hands of the children. If there is gluing to be done, the kids should be in charge of the glue bottles, and if materials need sorting and arranging, the kids should be doing the sorting and arranging.

Some of the prepackaged learning kits we looked at were also very scripted, telling the adult what to say and when to say it and even suggesting how to respond to expected questions. The curriculums seemed canned and expected robotic behavior from caregivers. Our biggest problem with these boxed kits, however, was that they often failed to give the children any actual experience with whatever the theme happened to be.

One ocean-themed activity never put kids near saltwater—or any water, for that matter. Instead, it directed children to paste precut sea creatures on blue paper. A weeklong fire-themed package never allowed children near real fire. The closest it came was a campfire constructed from blocks sprinkled with red, yellow, and orange strips of paper. Standing around a block-and-construction-paper campfire is *not* a real fire experience. It is not the same as standing near a real campfire: you feel no heat on your arms and face, you do not get smoke in your eyes, you do not hear the pop, snap, crackle, and sizzle of the flames, you do not get a sense of the power and danger of combustion, and you cannot cook a hot dog.

Don't feel safe with kids around a raging campfire? How about a candle? At least a candle's fire is real. You can hold your hand over the flame and feel its heat. You can roast a mini marshmallow on a toothpick. You can get some understanding of the danger and power of fire. An experience with a candle is a much more real fire experience than a pile of blocks and some construction paper scraps on the playroom floor. Fire safety should not be about keeping kids away from fire. It should be about teaching them to respect it. For that to happen, children need real experience with its real power in real life.

Phony block and construction paper fires are useful, however, in child-initiated dramatic play—after kids have had a *real* fire experience. Recreating fire on their own in this safe way does help kids hardwire their learning. It does help them understand and integrate the real experience into their life and knowledge base.

Which brings us to egg cartons.

One of the most offensive and fake activities we came across directed adults working with toddlers to put egg cartons on the floor and let the kids walk across them as . . . . wait for it . . . . wait for it . . . . SNOW EXPERIENCE.

Now, there is nothing wrong with letting toddlers walk on egg cartons. In fact, it sounds kind of fun. The kids could do it in their bare feet, and it would be a neat tactile experience and a chance to hone their balance. The egg cartons would make a nice noise as little feet smooshed them.

It is in no way, however, a snow experience.

Snow is cold. Egg cartons are not. Snow is wet. Egg cartons are not. Snow is to egg carton as giraffe is to jellybean. They are completely unalike.

Toddlers taking part in this activity learn nothing about snow. They walk away with no understanding of the texture, taste, or sound of snow. It's just a cutsie-wootsie wittle activity someone dreamed up for the babies and scrunched into a boxed curriculum.

Contrast that with a real first-time snow experience. I (Jeff) once met a young girl selling necklaces at the entrance to a black sand beach on the island of Hawaii. She was a bubbly, dark-haired, and talkative kid about twelve years old. We chatted for a long time, and after hearing I was from Iowa, she shared the story of her first snow experience.

She said that when she was littler, there had been a lot of snow up high on Mauna Loa, so her grandma and auntie loaded all the cousins into the truck and drove up the volcano until they reached the snow. She told me how they played in it, there on the chilly side of a tropical volcano. Then they piled as much of the snow as they could into the bed of the truck and hurried back down to the beach, where they had a snowball fight on the black sand beach.

This was a real experience with snow. The girl's deep brown eyes sparkled as she shared her story with me, and it would have been impossible to erase the smile from her face.

Real experiences build real memories and result in real learning. The girl from the black sand beach will remember and fondly recall her first snow experience for the entirety of her life. Do you think the eyes of toddlers taking part in an egg carton snow activity will sparkle years later when they recall the experience?

Here are some tips for keeping it real:

- **Whose hands are busy?** If *you're* doing a lot of work in preparation for an activity or project, it's probably not going to be a real experience for the children.

- **Do a smell test.** Step back from an activity you're planning and take a whiff. Does the activity smell real, or does it smell phony and contrived?

- **Pay attention.** The things children show interest in and are drawn to are going to lead to real experiences.

- **Remember that *real* does not necessarily mean *real exciting*.** The real things that kids are drawn to are often mundane and boring to adults: wiping tables after lunch, folding towels, counting forks.

SEE PROCESS OVER PRODUCT

It's not the cookies—it's the measuring, the mixing of ingredients, sweet smells, soft textures, sneakily licking batter from the spatula, and happy conversation.

It's not the picture—it's the trial-and-error to create just the right shades of color, the pushing of the brush across paper as your hands and eyes work together, the emergence of an image from inside your head into the world, the smell, feel, and maybe taste of the paint, and the feeling of joyous concentration.

It's not winning—it's how you play the game, who you play the game with, the exertion you put forth, the effort of your mind and body working seamlessly together, the bonding among peers, and the internal feeling of pride for a game well played.

It's not how well you sing—it's the fact that you open your mouth and put forth sound, the adding of your voice to the choir, the tingling you feel as many voices become one, and the in-the-moment awareness of your voice drifting out into the universe.

Early learning—and most everything else—works better when you focus on the here-and-now process instead of the off-in-the-future finished product. Part of trusting children to lead their own learning means leaving them to their processes and accepting that those may be a whole lot different from yours—which can be hard to do, because children's processes may not be as organized as you would like, sometimes take a lot more time than you expect, may be messier than you prefer, and are likely to go off in new and unexpected directions.

You may find not focusing on the finished product hard too. A lot of people think there needs to be something in the cubby or backpack at the end of the day to prove that children accomplished something. (And it had better be worthy of hanging on the refrigerator with the magnet Grandma brought back from Las Vegas.) People caught up in the finished product rather than the process tend to take over a lot of the process. They cut out the pieces, micromanage the positioning of the googly eyes, and urge the kids to keep the colors inside the lines.

Focusing on product over process steals a lot of learning opportunities from children. The way they learn to cut circles out of construction paper is to actually cut circles out of construction paper, not to have some good-intentioned adult do it for them so the caterpillar body looks good on the bulletin board.

Sometimes there may not be anything at all to hang up on the bulletin board. Some activities are all process: playing in the mud, climbing trees, building block towers, following bumblebees around the yard.

When you step back and let children control their own process, you'll learn a lot about them: where they are developmentally, what their interests are, and how their self-management skills are coming along. It's information that will be useful to you as you make plans to follow their lead in the future.

The finished product can be valuable too. Use it to help children self-evaluate. You can ask them questions about their play:

- Did that painting turn out the way you wanted it to? Why or why not?

- What would you like to do differently the next time we roast vegetables for lunch?

- How do you think we could make the next block tower taller?

Questions like these encourage children to think about their thinking, which is a higher-order skill.

Here are some ideas to help you focus on process over product:

- **Sit back and watch children at play; jot notes about what they're learning.** It's not always easy to see the learning that's going on, but with practice, you'll come to see that a simple activity like caring for a baby doll builds social skills, hand-eye coordination, language skills, kinesthetic awareness, leadership skills, large- and small-muscle control, prewriting skills, premath skills, and so much more. Seeing the learning will help you value the process.

- **Pay attention to your own process.** Focus on how you do what you do the next time you prepare yourself a meal or make the bed. Throw yourself into the process with the energy and focus of a two-year-old with fingerpaints. This sort of engagement in your own processes will help you understand the value in the doing.

- **Think about how you feel when someone takes over your process from you.** Doing so will help you better understand how kids feel when a well-intentioned adult jumps in and dictates the "right" way to do something.

MAKE *YES* EASY

Remember being four or eight or sixteen, asking something, and hearing the word *no*?

"Can I have a puppy? I promise to take care of it."

"No."

"Can I go to a party at Mary's house? Her parents aren't home, but her big brother agreed to chaperone. Please?"

"No."

The word *no* implies a lack of trust. It also restricts action, limits options, avoids risk, evades challenges, and prevents novel experiences. Another thing about the word *no* is that it doesn't work all that well, as anyone who has ever tried to keep a six-year-old out of a cookie jar or a sixteen-year-old away from a party can attest.

Yes is a word of exploration, challenge, risk, learning, adventure, and fun. *Yes* gets you a puppy, ice cream cone, or first kiss. *Yes* empowers.

Saying yes a lot also makes *no* more useful when you need it. If you use *no* only when you really need it, its effect will be more powerful, and the person you're saying it to is more likely to listen.

To empower children as learners and to show our trust in them, we need to shun no and make yes easy. We need to create environments and situations in which children can do as they please as much as possible. No should be reserved for real safety issues and real dangers. In the United States, knee-deep in the twenty-first century, we have an overblown expectation of safety—our modern lives are remarkably safe compared to those of generations past—just a hundred years ago, young children were working dangerous factory jobs in which it wasn't uncommon for them to be maimed by machinery—and we see danger around every corner. But when you think back to your own childhood, or to the childhoods of your parents and grandparents, you'll see that things considered "just too dangerous" now were commonplace then. What's more, past generations of children thrived.

Here are a couple of tips for identifying real safety issues and real dangers so you can say yes more often when considering activities and materials:

- **Consider your own childhood.** Was what you're considering for the children today safe enough for you back when you were a rug rat?

- **Ask yourself WWGGGTD**—What Would Great-Grandma Get to Do?

- **When you receive a no, take a skeptical look at who is telling you no, and why.** Sometimes there simply isn't a safety issue. Sometimes the authority figure can't actually come up with a logical, valid reason for having said no. And sometimes there isn't actually an authority figure saying no. Trainers hear all the time that this or that isn't allowed in a program because it's not safe, but sometimes, after looking into the safety issue, it turns out that such a rule doesn't exist. Recently during a training Jeff was doing on play, a caregiver said, "I'm sorry, these are great ideas, but the state will just not let us do these things. They're too dangerous." Before Jeff could respond, the head of child care licensing for the state stood up and said, "No, No, No! All of this is good stuff. We want you to do these things in your programs."

Letting Go of No

One of the big hang-ups many caregivers have when learning to put children in charge of the curriculum is letting go of no and making yes easy. Let's call it what it is: a control thing. We adults tend to like to be in control. We like to have people listen to us, do what we tell them to do, follow our instructions, do our bidding. We like to be The Boss, The Chief, The Big Kahuna, The Man, The Khan, The Captain, The Coach, The Czar, The Pasha, The General, The King, or The Queen. We like to push the buttons, pull the strings, make the rules, chart the course, compose the tune, and choreograph the dance. We like to have authority.

Unfortunately, saying no is more of a sign of authority for most adults than saying yes. We were probably hardwired for this as children when we consistently heard adults telling us no.

"Mommy, can I pet that puppy?"

"No."

"Daddy, can I make mud cupcakes with real sprinkles?"

"No."

"Grandpa, can we feed the ducks?"

"No."

For many of us, the first words we heard when we started walking and headed off to explore the world were something along the lines of "No! . . . Don't touch that, honey. . . . It's dangerous" or "No! . . . Icky. . . . Not in your mouth" or "No! . . . That's not for babies." From our earliest days, we learned to equate the word *no* with power, so it was only natural for us to grow up and put the word *no* in our I-Am-the-Authority toolbox. Over the years, we've come to rely on this tool more than we might realize. No becomes comfortable in our hands, it's always available, and it can be effective.

The problem with no is that while it may prove useful in controlling others, consolidating authority, avoiding a certain amount of chaos, and asserting power, it does little to empower others. Caregivers of children should shift from a *no* mind-set to a *yes* mind-set, because a caregiver's job is not to hoard power but to help children grow into powerful individuals. The job of early learning professionals and parents is not to *control children*, but to help children learn to *control themselves*.

Here's an example of the shift from no to yes in Jeff's family child care program:

From Jeff's World

For as long as I could remember, the rule for sand was that it was supposed to stay in the sandbox. Whenever we were outside, I would repeat the phrase "Keep the sand in the sandbox" dozens of times.

"Keep the sand in the sandbox."

"Keep the sand in the sandbox."

"Keep the sand in the sandbox."

"Keep the sand in the sandbox."

"Keep the sand in the sandbox."

"Keep the sand in the sandbox."

I really don't know why this was the rule. It just was. It was the rule at my house when I was a kid. It was the rule at all my friends' houses. It was the rule for my kids when they were little. It was the rule at every sandbox I ever encountered. Maybe it was to conserve the sand. Maybe it was to keep sand out of the surrounding area. Maybe it was just a control thing.

Anyway, saying, "Keep the sand in the sandbox," over and over was starting to cramp my style—there were more enjoyable things for me to do while we were outside than play sand cop. I also noticed it was certainly limiting play options for the kids. So I sat down on my thinking stump and did some thinking. Letting the children haul sand wherever they liked would open a completely new world of play; free me from playing sand cop; improve the drainage in my yard; and cost thirty dollars a year, at most, to top off the sandbox.

Nowadays sand can go wherever the kids want to take it. They haul it by the bucket or the teaspoonful across the yard. They scoop shovelfuls down the slide. They mix it with dirt and water and grass clippings, and flower petals and leaves and sticks and pinecones and mulch. They put it in their pockets. Mostly, though, they keep it within a few feet of the sandbox. Saying yes to sand outside the sandbox expanded the kids' learning and removed a stressor from my life, but most of all, it gave the children more control over their actions.

Obviously, caregivers can't say yes to everything, or some little person would cut the cat's hair every day, the toilet would be plugged with action figures and stuffed animals, and there would be a never-ending water balloon war in the living room. Shifting to a mind-set that allows a yes response to activities that aren't too dangerous or too unhealthy, to actions that don't make your head completely explode, and to adventures that aren't overly illegal or destructive will widen the world for kids and help them learn to manage their own power. For example, allowing kids to take sand *out* of the sandbox, climb *up* the slide, play with small objects that *could* be choked on, handle bugs and worms, pretend a stick is a gun, or make their own PB&J sandwiches are things you could say yes to. Don't worry, saying yes does not take your power away. You will find that empowering others only enhances their respect and admiration for you.

The shift from no to yes is generally not an easy one, but making a mindful effort to bring more yeses into your day will help turn yes into your new go-to answer. It will help change your hardwired habit for no into a new habit for yes. The more you say yes, the easier it becomes to keep saying yes—and to let go of no. With that in mind, we've pulled together some suggestions that may be helpful:

- **Look at your physical environment.** Take a hard look at your physical space and consider what changes you could implement to make a *Yes* mind-set easier than a *No* mind-set. For example, when the big kid puzzles are on a top shelf in the back of a closet, it's far easier for you to say no to puzzle time than yes. But when those puzzles are on a shelf in the main activity area where the big kids can reach them, it's a lot easier for you to say yes. Optimize your space so that yes can have a huge impact on the quality and amount of learning taking place.

- **Add more *yeses* to your day.** Constructing new habits is the foundation for shifting your mind-set. Unless your skin is green, you ride a broom, and you fear water and falling houses, you probably don't say no to everything. To change your mind-set, don't just focus on saying no less, but try to add more yeses to your day. Pay attention to the times you are already saying yes. For example, are you more prone to say yes in the morning, after everyone is settled in for the day, or in the afternoon, when the day is winding down? Are you more likely to say yes to quiet activities than loud ones? Pay attention to when and why you currently say yes, and then as your day unfolds, try to create more of these situations. For example, if you are more likely to say yes in the morning after your coffee, try to squeeze as many in as possible while the yes window is open.

- **If you don't really care, say yes.** If a request comes your way that you're generally ambivalent about, then answer yes. If you're just saying no out of habit and you really don't care either way, then why not answer yes? Does it really matter if you answer yes to questions like "Can we use the skinny markers instead of the fat ones?" or "Is it okay if we bring the blocks to the table?"

- **Add a *but* to your no.** Say no to the things you're not yet ready to say yes to, and then add the word *but* to your sentence to find an alternative way to achieve the children's goal. Here's an example:

  Child: Teacher, Teacher, can we color our feet with these markers?

  The old you: No, don't you dare! How did you get your hands on those markers anyway?

  The new you, adding a *but* to your no: No, *but* we can get out the washable paint and you can paint your feet or No, *but* we sure can use those markers to decorate the old wooden picnic table in the yard, if you can be careful with them.

Adding a *but* to your no also comes in handy when you feel a child's request is really too dangerous, unhealthy, annoying, or destructive. For example,

  "Hey, the hamster does *not* go in that slingshot again, *but* you can shoot these tinfoil balls."

  "Brady, honey, it's *not* good to stick green beans up your nose, *but* you can stuff them into this twisty straw."

- **Evaluate your big nos.** We all have a few big nos we hold tightly to—things we say no to out of habit, principle, or stubbornness. Here's an exercise that will help you evaluate your biggest nos.

Make a list of the three nos you'd have the hardest time letting go of, the things you say no to the most as an average day ticks by.

_____

_____

_____

Now, take a hard look at the list. Think about why you really say no to those things. Is it a power thing? Does it mean less cleanup later? Does it mean you won't have to get up and walk over to the supply closet? Is it just something you're in the habit of saying no to?

Notice how saying no to these things makes you feel. Do you feel powerful or guilty or ambivalent or bothered or _____ _____? (You fill in the blank.)

Next, ask yourself what would have to change to make the word yes more likely to pop out of your mouth. What would make yes a no-brainer for you? More pay? More staff? Fewer kids in the program?

_____

_____

_____

Last, how would it feel to be able to say yes to these things? Sit for a moment and visualize the last time you said no to each of the three big nos on your list, and then let yes scenarios play out in your head. Picture yourself being open to and supportive of the scenarios you habitually negate in real life.

This exercise will help you open up to the possibility of saying yes the next time you encounter one of your big nos. It might not make a yes as easy or as likely as a no, but it will give it a fighting chance.

The more you do to make saying yes easy while maintaining health, safety, and sanity, the better your learning environment will be for children. Shifts in mind-set aren't always easy, but they can be very beneficial.

Here are some ideas to help you make yes easier:

- How do you feel as an adult when you are arbitrarily told no by an authority figure?

- What three changes in the workplace would make yes easier for you?

- Compare how you feel when you say yes to how you feel when you say no. Which one feels better?

Building Relationships

Child care is about relationships. Building a strong emotional environment requires that you know every child as an individual and work to build a unique bond with him. The better you know the children, the better you can relate to them. For example, what's Freddie's favorite toy? What's Meg's home life like? How much sleep do the Kwon twins need, and how much do they actually get? How does baby Chloe express her need for attention? What things make Zeek shut down and withdraw?

Knowing children as individuals can help you manage those who are challenging, draw the ones who are quiet out of their shells, and keep in touch with others who are easy and sometimes get ignored. Knowing each child takes a lot of emotional labor, observation, and commitment, but tuning in to children as unique individuals pays off in the long run. The better you know each child, the easier it is to read, inspire, and work with each child.

SUPPORT WITH WORDS

We've touched on how *no* steals power and *yes* grants it, but what about other ways to use language to show children that we trust them as learners? We're not talking about praise here. What we are talking about are open-ended questions and empowering language.

Open-ended questions require not only more thought on the part of the caregiver but also the use of more words. Hearing more words builds vocabulary and speaking skills in children and shows them that the questioner values their opinions, implying trust. Here are examples of open-ended questions:

- What are you going to do next?

- How could we make the color green?

- What shall we eat for snack?

- Who do you think is coming in the door?

- Where should we hang the bird feeder?

- When do you think the snow will melt?

- Why do you think the tree's shadow moves during the day?

Using open-ended questions when you communicate with a child helps you get to know her mind a bit better, too, and when you know the individual child, you can better set the stage for future learning, notice developmental concerns, and deepen your relationship.

Now here are some examples of what we mean by empowering language:

- You can . . .

- You work at . . .

- You do your best to . . .

- You attempt to . . .

- You choose . . .

- You create . . .

- You know . . .

- You do . . .

When you use these supportive *You* phrases, you help young children engage their worlds, knowing that they have your support and trust. With a little effort, you can weave empowering language into your conversations with children. We could have written these empowering *You* phrases as complete sentences, but the truth is that what comes next doesn't matter nearly as much as those first few empowering *You* words. Using empowering language will help kids take the lead in their own learning and open them to more exploration and discovery.

Here are some tips for using supportive words to trust kids as learners:

- **Catch kids exhibiting behaviors you value and then tell them you value their efforts.** "Claudia, you are working so hard on that bug puzzle"; "Ming, you really stood up for yourself when Raul and Abraham were trying to take the ball from you."

- **Seek out opportunities to ask open-ended questions.** If you pay attention, you will find more moments when you can sneak a question or two into the day. "Can you tell me why you did that?" is a great question to ask before jumping to conclusions. "How are we going to fix this?" is a useful question when a child breaks something.

- **Consider creating a cheat sheet.** Child care is often fast paced and hectic, so there's nothing wrong with carrying an index card of open-ended questions and *You* phrases in your pocket. If carrying a cheat sheet of empowering language helps you work more of it into your day, then do it until it becomes habit.

BACK OFF A BIT

Sometimes adults hover. It's well-intentioned hovering, but it's not as helpful as they think. Being *right there* for kids all the time does not encourage them to take risks, find their own solutions, develop their social skills, self-regulate, and learn to know themselves. It also leaves them thinking the world is overly dangerous, they aren't up to its challenges, and they aren't trusted to make good choices. Child care providers like to talk about *helicopter parents*—the ones who are always hovering, ready to swoop in and rescue their children—or *snowplow parents*—the ones who are always out in front, clearing the path for their kids—but we see a lot of *helicopter caregivers* and *snowplow caregivers* too. We're not knocking these grown-ups—in fact, we have been these grown-ups. The truth is, though, that kids are more capable than adults give them credit for, and sometimes adults do too much for them. It seems safer, more efficient, and easier (for the adults) to step in. And always being nearby and ready to lend a hand means things will get done right (right = the grown-up's way), but it steals lots of learning moments from children.

Don't think you're a helicopter or a snowplow? Consider the following:

- **Have you ever told a child how to feel?** "You hit Missy, and you should feel sorry for that! Go tell her you're sorry—*and mean it.*"

133

- **Have you ever made a decision for a child that he was capable of making for himself?** "Do you want an apple or an orange? These apples look good. Let's cut up an apple!"

- **Have you ever micromanaged a child's activity or routine?** "No, no, honey. You should glue the fishy's eyes on the other side. You're putting them by her tail. Silly boy, fishies don't have eyes on their tails!"

- **Have you ever just done it yourself?** Do you ever put on or tie a child's shoes because it is quicker than letting her do it herself? Do you ever pick up the toys so everything gets put exactly where you want it? Do you ever cut out the project pieces or do the hard parts of an activity to smooth the way?

Over time, this sort of hovering and snowplowing disempowers children. It steals their learning moments. Back off a bit, and when you do, you'll discover two additional benefits: *necessary* roughness and *nurtured* rebellion.

Necessary Roughness

Aggressive physical play is good for children, but adults try to stop it because it seems violent, inappropriate, disorderly, and valueless. According to Stuart Brown in *Play: How It Shapes the Brain, Opens the Imagination, and Invigorates the Soul,*

> Research on rough-and-tumble play in animals and humans has shown that it is necessary for the development and maintenance of social awareness, cooperation, fairness, and altruism. Its nature and importance are generally unappreciated, particularly by preschool teachers or anxious parents, who often see normal rough-and-tumble play behavior such as hitting, diving, and wrestling (all done with a smile, between friends who stay friends) not as a state of play, but a state of anarchy that must be controlled. Lack of experience with rough-and-tumble play hampers the normal give-and-take necessary for social mastery, and has been linked to poor control of violent impulses in later life (2009, 1013).

We would never stop a flock of puppies or a herd of kittens from engaging in rough-and-tumble play, but we do it to children all the time. Brown also writes that war play and other violently themed or aggressive play are part of childhood and help kids develop social skills, understand aggression, learn to self-regulate, and deal with their fears. There is a distinct difference between real aggression and real violence and play aggression and play violence, and kids see it clearly.

Nurtured Rebellion

Our world needs more free spirits, open-minded thinkers, rebels, and outlaws willing to dance to their own groove, shake things up, see from a different perspective, fight the system, innovate, stand tall in the face of tyranny, hold their ground, and face the Goliaths they encounter. Our factory-model school educational system sucks rebellion out of children. An (un)curriculum should nurture it. We're not talking about rebellion for the sake of rebellion or rebellion that grows from boredom. Nor are we talking about self-serving or selfish rebellion. We're talking about the altruistic, brave rebellion that Martin Luther King Jr., Mohandas Gandhi, Lucy Stone, Thomas Jefferson, and Luke Skywalker had, and when you see it in children, we want you to nurture it.

Here are tips for backing off a bit so you can allow some necessary roughness and nurtured rebellion:

- Evaluate your policies and procedures and look at ways to codify rough-and-tumble play.

- Create space in your physical environment for rough-and-tumble play.

- Educate parents about the value of rough-and-tumble play.

- Accept aggressive and violently themed play. It helps build healthy brains, and besides, if you've ever tried to prevent it, you know that's about as difficult to do as slowing the sunrise.

- Let children know that you respect their tenacity and stubbornness, even if these traits are hard to live with sometimes.

- Create opportunities for children to step up, be leaders, and make hard choices.

- Support the interests of outcasts and kids who swim against the prevailing current.

- Allow children to make their own choices and then live with the natural consequence of those choices.

NUDGE WHEN NEEDED

Hovering and snowplowing can hinder learning, but every once in a while, children need a nudge to help them build new skills and understanding. We've all seen mommy birds push their babies from the nest to get them to fly, or dog mommies wean their pups by walking away. Children need these supportive and timely nudges too. Knowing when to step in and suggest a course of action ("Maybe if you build the base of your tower like this, it will be stabler"), when to offer an insight ("You look sad—I feel sad sometimes when I say something mean to a friend too"), when to share a new word ("Those are called pinecones; most people don't pick them up off the ground and then eat them like that"), and when to walk away ("I'm going to let you figure this one out on your own") are valuable skills.

While caregivers should stand back and let children do things for themselves, they still need to keep an eye on the children's activities, observing their learning, noting potential developmental concerns, and anticipating needs. Caregivers need to watch for moments when challenging struggles between children become too stressful, as well as for the subtle signals children give indicating that help, suggestions, or intervention is welcome.

Here are some tips to help your nudging:

- **Lend a hand.** You can step in to lend a hand ("Can I help you with that button?"); demonstrate a skill ("Want to see how I like to tie my shoe?"); offer an encouraging word ("Can I tell you something? I like how hard you are working on that painting!"); share an insight ("Can I show you a way to make your block tower stronger?"); or suggest a different course of action ("Can you think of something to do besides spit the next time Leroy pulls your hair? Would telling him in your serious voice that you don't like it work better?").

- **Give children the help they want, not the help you think they need.** Remember that your focus should be on the child's learning, not on your teaching. If Samantha is fiddling with her shoelaces but decides she doesn't want to see how a shoe is tied when you offer, let her know she can come to you later if she changes her mind, and allow her to continue her efforts. If she decides she wants your help later, give her just as much as you sense she needs and then leave her to her work.

- **Praise effort.** When you offer encouragement, praise a specific effort, not the general result. Encouragement of this sort focuses attention on the value of trying rather than on the result. Praising effort is a way to take away pressure and give value to imperfect results.

EMBRACE MISTAKES

The ongoing rush through childhood and the obsession with academic assessment brought on by No Child Left Behind, Kids Getting Older Younger, and adult fear have created a generation of children afraid to make mistakes. Mistakes are seen as failures, and to quote the remarkable Ron Howard movie *Apollo 13*, "Failure is not an option." The fear of making mistakes (and of disappointing the people who love them) keeps many children boxed up and unwilling to explore, try new things, and follow their whims and desires. Fear of failure isn't a problem for infants and one-year-olds, but sometime between learning to talk and the first day of kindergarten, many children become socialized to fear making mistakes. And if it hasn't happened by their first day of kindergarten, it will happen soon enough for the majority of children.

Help young children embrace their mistakes. Mistakes, after all, are our attempts to know the world. After we make a mistake, we know something that we didn't know before—that's a good thing. Our brains are built to learn from the mistakes we make, so instead of cowering in fear from them, we need to stand up and bravely embrace them.

If you need an example of embracing mistakes to bring the idea home, visualize that one- or two-month window when a mobile infant goes from taking her very first steps to becoming a walker: lots of falling, some crying, missteps, forehead bumps, and plenty of mistakes, but in a very short time, she is confidently zipping along, giggling, and turning corners like a Ferrari on a closed track—all while carrying a block in one hand and a stuffed pig in the other. Mistakes are powerful teachers.

Taking away the fear of making mistakes will help children relax, limber up, be a bit sillier, take things less seriously, and, most important, take more chances. These things, brain research tells us, lead to more learning, better retention, and stronger neural pathways, and they also make childhood a lot more fun.

Here are some useful tips for embracing mistakes:

- **Ignore them.** Bite your tongue and control your body language. Don't acknowledge failed efforts as mistakes. Don't say things like "Oh my, you really messed up this time," or give *that look* (you know the one; it's probably the same one your mom or dad or aunt Sadie gave you when you were growing up). Don't correct or offer unsolicited advice using sentences that start with "Next time . . .," "I would . . .," "You should . . .," "It would be better if . . .," or "This is the way you should. . . ." Don't act like the world is going to end because a two-year-old spills milk. Spilled milk will not cause a thermonuclear meltdown of the earth's core, it does not influence the time/space continuum, and the alien army cloaked just above our atmosphere will not attack because Bennie tipped a cup. Milk is easy to clean up, there are plenty of cows to make more, and the only way little Bennie is going to master using a cup so she can one day put on her electric boots and a mohair suit and go out drinking with the Jets after a concert is to spill a few times.

- **Think about how you feel when you make a mistake.** If you're thinking *How will they know they made a mistake if I don't point it out?* or *How will they do it right next time if I don't tell them now?*, take a moment and think about your own life. When have you needed other people to point out your mistakes? Do you enjoy having someone offer unsolicited advice on how to do it right? Talk about your mistakes with the children. Let them into your world so they know you're not perfect and that imperfection is okay. This will take the pressure off them, reduce the fear of making mistakes, and create an atmosphere supportive of exploration and taking risks. Real, honest conversation is a powerful teacher.

AVOID AWARDS AND PRAISE

Awarding children for following rules and praising them for their achievements may seem innocuous, but awards and praise actually work against our efforts to help children prepare to function in the adult world. Rewards like stickers and juice boxes can weaken children because they impede developing self-regulation skills, and praise makes it harder for children to take risks, try new things, face challenges, and stick out their necks. Rewards and praise can cripple children by putting them into a success-is-the-only-goal box and clouding their thinking.

Stickers

Stickers can make life easier for adults, but they infringe on children's ability to self-regulate. A big part of humans developing self-control is finding our intrinsic motivation: we learn to do things because we sense they are the right things to do, and we avoid doing the things we sense are wrong. Becoming dependent on extrinsic rewards like stickers hinders development of our intrinsic, autonomous motivation. Picking up toys because it is the right thing to do is not the same as picking up toys to get a princess sticker. Stickers and other awards adults give kids can become addictive. We've actually seen groups of three- and four-year-olds wandering the streets looking for a hit. "Hey, dude . . . I gotta get right. . . . Are you holding? . . . Maybe a little Dora, or a gold star? . . . I'm really jonesing here. . . . I'll pay. . . . I'll, like, go potty or pick up some toys, or use my manners when Grandma comes. . . . Whatever it takes."

Think we're exaggerating? Of course we are, but not much. The anticipation of those stickers releases dopamine into a part of the brain known as the nucleus accumbens, which is the brain's pleasure center and the same area of the brain that is believed to play an important part in addictive behavior. Mmmmmm . . . dopamine.

Compliments

Research shows that praising children for their achievements, telling them how smart they are, or fawning over how pretty they are cripples them and takes away their willingness to take risks, face new challenges, and move out of their comfort boxes. If for as long as you remember everyone has been telling you how smart you are, and then you take a risk that results in a mistake, what happens to your self-image? If all you hear are compliments about how cute and pretty you are, why should you make an effort to be anything more than that? Why focus on your inner strengths when everyone else is focused on your outward appearance?

The stress and anxiety resulting from praise can also influence the kind of lifelong learners children become. In an e-mail message (January 18, 2010) to us, Peter Gray writes, "People do become lifelong learners because that is human nature, not because of the educational system. In fact, in their lifelong learning, people tend to avoid the subjects that were taught in school—such as math, history, and so on—because they associate them with stress and anxiety. If we could focus more attention on the personal effort children exert and the intrinsic value of learning and self-discovery instead of praise and rewards, then children might not become so disheartened by topics such as math, reading, and science in school. Evolution has wired us to learn throughout life, but inappropriate rewards and praise throw up roadblocks that turn many away from learning.

Results-oriented rewards and praise and the implied need for perfection associated with them in the early years of life have led a lot of young people to rebel, melt down, and self-injure when they reach their late teens and early twenties. You can learn more about this by checking out the Research tab at www.challengesuccess.org. Compliments do not show children that they are trusted to lead their own learning. "When a parent or other caregiver expects too much of any child," write Margaret B. Puckett and Janet K. Black in *Understanding Toddler Development*, "healthy growth and development can be slowed and the relationship harmed" (2007, 37).

To show children that we trust them, we need to abandon awards and bribes and trust that they can build self-regulation skills. We also need to pay close attention to *how* we praise. Praising *effort* rather than accomplishment—"Wow, you worked hard on that project" or "I could really see you concentrating on that structure you were building" or "You were so careful while climbing the apple tree"—empowers.

Here are some tips for avoiding awards and praise:

- Toss out your sticker charts and quit handing out jelly beans after the toys are picked up.

- Look for opportunities to praise effort.

- Investigate this topic more and check out these books:

  A Nation of Wimps: The High Cost of Invasive Parenting by Hara Estroff Marano

  NurtureShock: New Thinking about Children by Po Bronson and Ashley Merryman

  The website of parenting expert John Rosemond (www.rosemond.com)

It seems counterintuitive that awards and praise can actually diminish learning, exploration, and creativity in young children—our society, after all, is driven by them. Nevertheless, programs offering an (un)curriculum should shift their focus from offering these extrinsic rewards and help children stay in touch with their intrinsic drive to learn and understand.

Because young children are so new to the world and so limited in experience, it also seems counterintuitive to trust them to direct their own learning, but the drive to learn is inborn and powerful. Early learning programs are much more effective—and fun—when they stop fighting this innate drive and start trusting children as thoughtful, engaged, and passionate learners.

(Un)Planning

We do not have to worry about curricula, lesson plans, motivating children to learn, testing them, and all the rest that comes under the rubric of pedagogy. Let's turn that energy, instead, toward creating decent environments in which children can play. Children's education is children's responsibility, not ours. Only they can do it. They are built to do it. Our task regarding education is just to stand back and let it happen. The more we try to control it, the more we interfere.

—Peter Gray, "Children Educate Themselves I: Outline of Some of the Evidence"

The evolution of the human brain changed everything. For the first time, there was an animal that could think about how it thought. . . . We could tell elaborate lies and make plans for the future. Sometimes, we could even follow our plans.

—Jonah Lehrer, *How We Decide*

Our amazing brains can be a curse. Our ability to think about how we think and to plan for future events are very powerful mental tools, but the cold hard fact is that our ability to do these things evolved over millions of years of dealing with spontaneity, randomness, serendipity, and novelty. Our brains are good at planning, predicting, and preparing precisely because our ancestors' brains dealt daily with the unpredictable, the uncertain, and the unknown.

Another cold, hard truth is that our minds are still fed by the spontaneity, novelty, and challenge of everyday interactions with the world. Sadly, not much attention is paid to our need for spontaneity when we plan experiences for children. Adult minds are most comfortable when the world is planned, organized, tidy, and orderly, but children's hungry minds quiver with delight at the idea of the unknown. Children are born eager to learn, and sometimes our well-intended planning gets in the way. To some, Peter Gray's thoughts on children's self-education may be very controversial, but the last thirty years of brain research backs them up.

Let's look at lesson and activity planning in terms of baking a cake. In traditional lesson or activity planning, you are a baker of sorts.

- You decide what kind of cake you're going to make.

- You choose the kind of cake that everyone is going to eat.

- You look over some tried-and-true recipes and select which one to use.

- You ensure the right tools are on hand: mixer, spatula, spoons, measuring cups—check, check, check, check.

- You anticipate the potential problems—"What will I do if eggshell gets in the batter?" "What if I spill on myself?"—and then try to avoid them—"I'll crack the eggs in a separate bowl before adding them to the rest of the mix." "I'd better wear that new apron I got for my birthday."

- You organize and mix the ingredients.

- You warm the oven and prepare the pan just so.

- You mix everything together, pop it in the oven, and hope it turns out.

This is how early childhood folks typically think about planning a curriculum. They decide what activity to present. They prepare the environment and make sure they have everything they need. They try to anticipate problems. With traditional activity or lesson planning, the early childhood caregiver is ultimately in charge of the project.

Planning in an (un)curriculum is not like baking a cake by yourself. It's more like assisting six or eight or twelve or twenty individual bakers as each follows her own unique recipe to make the exact kind of cake she's in the mood for. In fact, everyone may not be making cake: three of four are making cake, and one is busy preparing muffins, a couple others are baking cookies, two are making pizza, and that one over in the corner by herself is rebuilding a transmission.

Some of the bakers you are assisting may choose to bake the same thing over and over again for days on end. They are very meticulous about their process and don't like interference. Others need to start a new recipe every five minutes, and they consume lots of your supplies and time. Many don't even follow a recipe; they just slap ingredients together in order to create something that has never been created before. When they're done, they might have a cake, they might have a pie, or they might have a big stuck mess they can't clean up by themselves. Some of these bakers are very clingy and need a lot from you. Others want independence. They may come to you if they have problems, but then again, they may not.

In this kitchen, meticulous planning skills will get you only so far. Neatly written recipe cards may prove useless. Instead of planning and implementing, your job is to have plenty of ingredients on hand and a wide variety of utensils and equipment available. You need to be flexible enough to change from one recipe to another at the flick of a whisk. You need to be able to hand your little bakers what they need when they decide they need it. Better yet, you need to anticipate their needs.

In a traditional early learning environment, planning and preparation bring form to the caregiver's day, but in an (un)curriculum, caregivers need to plan for curiosity, challenge, and spontaneity—and then relax and see where these things take you. This isn't easy, as you probably know, because curiosity killed the cat, challenge can be so darn . . . well . . . challenging, and spontaneity is so . . . Oh, look, a butterfly!

From Denita's World

A was one of the last letters remaining. Every other letter had come up in conversation or discovery over the past months, and we'd expanded on them.

I'd just gotten a new book titled *Counting with Apollo* by Caroline Grégoire. The *A* in *Apollo* stood out on the cover, and the kids noticed it and pointed out the fact that we hadn't yet learned about *A*. And so the conversation began before we'd even opened the book.

145

"I know what starts with *A*, Nita! Apple!"

I quickly replied, "Hold on! Don't say any more. Let me grab my marker." I'm a firm believer in writing down what's being said when a child says it.

But as the spewing of words slowed, I was surprised by how small our list was: *apple*, *airplane*, *achoo*, and *animal*. I got out our trusty dictionary to give clues to more words the kids might know. *Absorb* was one of the first words that caught my eye. I knew they probably didn't know it, but they could certainly understand it. After adding the word to our list, I got a cup of water and a roll of paper towel for some hands-on exploration of the word.

We all crammed around a table. I gave Ella the cup of water and told her to dump it on the table. You should have seen her eyes light up at the prospect of purposeful spilling! I tore off a piece of paper towel and laid it on top of the water. We watched as a wet spot grew on the paper towel, and then I picked it up to reveal the dry table beneath. "That is called *absorb*," I told the kids.

"Do it again, Nita," they all said. So I filled the cup, handed it to another child, and he repeated the process. We did this again . . . and again . . . and again.

Finally, Jack said, "Can we put color in the water?" Of course we can! I grabbed some yellow liquid watercolor from the cupboard, filled the cup, added some of the color, handed it to another child, and repeated the process. Gasps followed, and then "Do it again." After three or so more times spilling with yellow, Parker suggested we do two spills: one yellow, and one blue. Yes! I grabbed a second cup, and we made blue water. Then two kids got to spill the colored water (which was turning out to be just as much fun as the absorption itself), and the two spills produced two separate circles (well, more like blobs) on the paper towel. Again, and again, we spilled and absorbed yellow and blue. I was tickled by how excited this simple activity made the children.

Then it happened—the most amazing accident ever! Picture this: a rectangular piece of paper towel, at one end a blob of yellow, at the other end a blob of blue. I picked up the paper towel, as I had done at least twenty-five times by this point, to throw it away. A child with a question stopped me in the process. As I talked to the child, holding the paper towel by one end, yellow at the top, blue at the bottom, the rest of the crew started jumping and cheering and yelling. "Look! Look! Look, Nita!" "It's moving! It's making *green*!" And then from Jack came, "Nita! This is *amaaaazing*!"

I decided to give the children free rein now. I filled bowls with colored water and got the pipettes out for more precise spilling. It didn't take long before kids were exploring with three colors and even having races! Two children worked together, squirting colored water at one end of the paper towel. Then they lifted the paper towel up and watched their color travel to the other end of the paper towel and drip onto the table. "Red is first! Red is first! But yellow is going to be second! No, wait, blue is going to beat yellow! Yellow will be last!" Again, again, and again they cheered their favorite colors on and predicted the outcomes of color races. The rest is history.

Can you see all the learning going on? The children were observing two things being mixed together and causing a change; they were observing gravity; they were working cooperatively; they were problem solving; they were using new vocabulary words, connecting a real-life moment to a new word; they were using math skills; and they were using observations to predict outcomes. A simple, spontaneous moment inspired hours of investigation, challenges, curiosity, and pure fun.

By the way, we never did read *Counting with Apollo*. We got so absorbed in absorption that the morning, filled with curiosity, challenge, and spontaneity, simply flew by.

Consider the following:

How do children usually respond to your well-planned lessons?

_____

_____

_____

Describe the last time you were spontaneous. (If you can't think of the last time, then quick, right now, go outside with no shoes on and run around the building. Drop to the ground every few yards and wave

your arms and legs in the air like a dying cockroach. Now describe
how you feel.)

_____

_____

_____

Think of two personal childhood moments: in one, you're busy with
an activity of your own choosing, and in the other, you're busy with an
adult-planned activity. Which was more engaging then and brings fonder
memories now, and why? (Relax. There are no right or wrong answers.)

_____

_____

_____

How did you feel after facing the last big challenge life tossed your way?

_____

_____

_____

When was the last time you let your curiosity get the better of you, and
what happened?

_____

_____

_____

Do you like to be told what to do, or do you like to have the freedom to
choose?

_____

_____

Throw Away Your Lesson Plan Book

No, that is not a typo.

Let's get real. For most people, preparing formal lesson plans for a bunch of kids is no trip to the beach on a sunny day with a cooler full of adult beverages and junk food. Sure, some people like lesson planning, but some people probably also like eating grilled pickle, squid, and lard sandwiches.

What happens when most grown-ups look at a blank lesson plan template like this?

Mouths get dry, hearts race, and the urge to immediately go do something fun like lick a shopping cart wheel or juggle grouchy tarantulas overwhelms.

Many early childhood educators were taught that formal lesson planning is the thing to do. Lots of people with fancy letters behind their names think

---

Lesson Plan Template

Lesson Plan Title: _____

Concept/Topic to Teach: _____

Standards Addressed: _____

General Goals: _____

Specific Objectives: _____

Materials Needed: _____

Related Books and Music: _____

Lead-in: _____

Procedures: _____

Closure: _____

Assessment: _____

Connections to Other Concepts/Topics: _____

---

it's important. But the truth is that most experienced caregivers find it tedious and unrewarding busywork. Lessons seldom unfold as planned, because it's statistically improbable that a given group of children will all be interested in the topic of the lesson at the same time that the provider is ready to present said lesson. You can use your bestest singsongy-happy voice; you can paste on your biggest I'm-excited-to-do-this face; and you can scold, growl, and snarl the children into compliance, but you can't make them all excited and obedient if they're not interested.

Remember, no matter how well planned and implemented, pre-planned usually feels contrived, forced, and phony, even to the person in charge of contriving the forced phoniness, when compared to an organic learning moment that grows from a real experience. Lesson planning also eats up a lot of time, because after you fill out the official lesson plan form, you have to pull together all the materials, move the children into the activity, do the activity, handle the kid who decided to glue his left eye shut while you were giving directions, move the children to the next planned learning event, deal with cleanup, and so on.

Not quite convinced? Here are eight more reasons never to do a lesson plan again:

1. Lesson planning feeds the hungry, fear-based, overscheduled, academics-instead-of-play, pressure-cooker beast that so many adults have rumbling under their beds and hiding in their closets. When adults plan lessons, they stop trusting the innate power of play to wire young brains.

2. Lesson plans typically focus on a small range of academic expectations like numeracy and literacy, failing to address the developmental needs of the whole child.

3. Lesson plans often come across as forced learning experiences that hinder imagination, stifle creativity, and make kids dependent on the adult. Nothing goes against fostering independence, imagination and creativity more than lesson plans.

4. Lesson planning leads to thoughtless, predictable, and rote activities created by adults who are often just going through the motions, doing what's expected of them. In turn, this leads to busy young brains that aren't challenged or fed the novelty they crave.

5. Lesson planning is seldom done solely for the children. Caregivers plan to make the boss happy, keep funding streams flowing, make parents happy, impress the quality-rating system evaluator, and not upset the custodian. They also plan with the clock and the calendar in mind. Such planning steals focus from the needs of the children.

6. Lesson plans are rarely in sync with the developmental needs of the children. Plan in November for an activity you'll do in January, and of course you'll miss the in-the-moment developmental needs of many, if not most, of the children.

7. Lesson planning can be stressful, overwhelming, and unfulfilling for the planner. The busywork that comes with planning sucks up a

lot of time, energy, and resources and leaves the planner drained. All these wrong reasons can really burn out a caregiver after a few years.

8. Lesson planning in early childhood programs is a relatively new import from higher education, and while lesson planning might make sense for high school and college students, young children have done fine without it for, oh, the first three or four million years of human evolution.

We're not saying planning and preparation are bad—they are vital and necessary. In fact, they're probably more necessary in a program using an (un)curriculum than they are in a traditional program. What we are saying is this: you need to step back from your usual way of doing things (lesson plans) and see other ways to plan and prepare. Simply knowing the children's interest is the simplest way of preparing. Know what to have on hand that can be grabbed at a moment's notice. Be organized and ready for the season, holiday, and the various discoveries that come with them. Depending too heavily on a lesson plan or boxed curriculum to tell you what and when to learn disempowers you and the children. Planning becomes a problem when you plan without listening to the children.

Changing the way you plan and prepare may be hard because change is scary and requires you to alter habits. As a responsible caregiver, though, you must face your fears and do what's right for the children.

From Denita's World

O how I loved my lesson plan book, especially when I had it all filled out, ready for the learning to begin. Its crinkly pages, full of lots and lots of activities I wanted to do, made me feel in control and prepared.

It was fall, the beginning of the school year, when real learning happened. We were going to begin exploring our senses. I had it all planned out: sense of touch, sight, smell, sound, and finally taste. We would learn about our senses for two weeks, and by the end the children would be able to identify the five senses by themselves. I had my objectives written out in an organized fashion. The children would be able to tell me what sense the nose was responsible for. The children would be able to . . . blah blah blah.

My plans were going smoothly until, lo and behold, we discovered a caterpillar living innocently in a sedum plant one day. The children became obsessed with the caterpillar, and our senses became a thing of the past. "Can we keep it? Please, Nita? Can we keep it?" They wanted me to get a jar and a stick.

Do you know how I responded? I said, with as much enthusiasm as a person could muster for the human nose, "Well, boys and girls, today we're going to learn about our (insert dramatic intonation) noses! In two weeks, just two, we'll get to learn about caterpillars (I had already written this in ink in my lesson plan book), and then we will find a caterpillar and keep him." The children actually deflated, and then they turned away.

This was my aha! moment. I stopped and thought to myself, *What are you doing? Good grief, Denita, keep the caterpillar! Learn about caterpillars now! Our senses aren't going anywhere. They'll still be here next week, or even next month.* This was hard for me to do, because it meant scribbling out and rewriting a part of my nice new planning book.

So I followed the children's lead, and we kept the caterpillar. I was able to squeeze in some conversation about our senses, too, when we read *The Very Hungry Caterpillar*. I made a sign-up sheet, and each of my child care families could choose something from the story they'd like to bring. We tasted salami, apple pie, Swiss cheese, pickles, and lollipops, to name a few. We experienced sour, sweet, salty, tangy, and bland.

The story of my aha! moment holds a special place in my heart, because it truly was a moment that changed me and my program forever. Sure, I still plan, but I do it in my head, where things can be, and often are, easily rearranged. I follow the children's lead and then do my best to provide opportunities that encourage and support their self-exploration, adventure, curiosity, challenges, self-esteem, and cooperation. No other kind of learning is funner, more open to possibilities, and, most important, more memorable for the children.

Be an Early Learning Experience Architect

To an outside observer, an unplanned environment may at times look chaotic and unstructured. Folks who do not know what play-based learning looks like have a hard time seeing it. To them, the scattered toys, the noise, and the motion make no sense. This may sound counterintuitive, but (un)planning takes a lot of planning. Mindful caregivers devote a lot of thought and preparation to creating (un)planned learning moments. We decided the folks doing this mindful (un)planning needed a job title. The one we came up with was *experience architect*.

We came across the phrase *experience architect* in Thomas Kelley's book *The Ten Faces of Innovation: IDEO's Strategies for Beating the Devil's Advocate and Driving Creativity throughout Your Organization*. In the business world, experience architects are the people who design the physical and emotional experiences you have when you interact with Google, Starbucks, or your iPod. They pay attention to things like how many clicks it takes you to find the online information you're looking for, the aroma you smell in a coffee shop, and the sleek feel of a well-designed electronic device in your hand. The job of the experience architect is to design experiences that fill a need.

Don't think this is important? Have you ever abandoned a website because you couldn't find what you were looking for or because the ads were making you nauseated? Have you ever decided not to eat in a restaurant because it didn't look clean, or started shopping at a new store because it seemed friendly and inviting? Experience architects consider the needs of customers and then try to create environments that fulfill those needs.

We decided to appropriate this term for the early learning profession. Give up your lesson planning templates and forgo the boxed curriculums—be an early learning experience architect instead. After all, at its core, your job is to create emotional and physical experiences for children based on their changing individual needs and interests.

One of the important things experience architects do is to find the core of an experience or interaction. In your work with children, you can ask yourself: "In this situation, what is the *necessary experience*?"

Take painting a picture, for example. Is the *picture you paint* the necessary experience? Perhaps it will be a masterpiece. Or is the *process of painting the picture* the necessary experience? Feeling the paint, observing the paint smearing across the paper and mingling with the other colors. Organizing muscles to move the paintbrush across the paper. Coordinating the eyes and hands to place the paint where they want it. Feeling the pleasure (or, depending on the child, the displeasure) of cold, slimy paint with their fingers.

Of course it's the process that's necessary. And it's your job as an early learning experience architect to know which experiences are the necessary ones—that is, which experiences are at the core of what young children need to feed their growing brains—and then to find a way to chip away everything else so children have the time, materials, attention, and support they need to experience them. As an early learning experience architect, you need to focus on finding the necessary experiences to feed the unique, in-the-moment needs of the children in your care.

Practice the Principles of (Un)Planning

The rest of this chapter is devoted to six ways of being that will help you (un)plan experiences for the children in your care. Here are the six principles of (un)planning:

- Be reactive.

- Be proactive.

- Be spontaneous.

- Be flexible.

- Be observant.

- Be relaxed.

Consider these simple but frequently overlooked ways of being as tools to help you design child-led learning experiences.

Knowing Yourself Helps You Connect to Children

Taking some time to know yourself a bit better can help improve your interactions with children as well as your depth of connection to them. Consider answering the following:

Are you a visual, auditory, or kinesthetic learner?

_____

_____

What is your temperament?

_____

_____

_____

What is your early learning philosophy?

_____

_____

What do you need from you interactions with children?

_____

_____

When do you have the most energy during the day?

_____

_____

What part of your workday is most challenging?

_____

_____

What part of your workday is most fulfilling?

_____

_____

What three things can swing your mood from good to bad?

_____

_____

What makes you feel better when you are down?

_____

_____

BE REACTIVE

Reactive is a tendency to react to events and situations instead of initiating or instigating them. Honing a reactive approach to lesson planning is key in an (un)curriculum. (Formal lesson planning tends to be the opposite of what we're looking for here.) Instead of initiating, instigating, or preplanning activities, let child-led play, exploration, and discovery happen—and *then* react appropriately. Plan for unplanned, unrehearsed, and uninitiated learning by paying attention to the objects, situations, textures, sounds, and other stimuli that make a child's eyes sparkle or consume her attention. Really listen to the children's questions and conversations, and notice what tugs at their attention. Then react by sharing materials or building situations that feed their interests and help them make discoveries. The two-year-old who is frequently found elbow-deep in the toilet probably has a very real and immediate interest in water. You can react to his interest by scolding him, or you can build some more appropriate water play for him.

Caregivers are often so busy, rushed, and overwhelmed that they either fail to notice what's drawing the children's attention or they gloss right over it. Rushing to get lunch on the table often means missing a chance to watch particles of dust dancing in the beam of sunlight bursting through the dining room window. Feeling overwhelmed by the growing stack of paperwork on your desk can cause you to miss the teachable moment when two children begin to argue over who will be the daddy in a game of house. The best thing to do in such a situation is to take a breath, slow down, and focus on seeing learning.

From Denita's World

One fine, cloudy, muggy day in June, I just knew it was going to rain. I was eager to get the children outside for some fresh air and a chance to burn off excess energy before it did. The minute we hit that outside air, one of the kiddos exclaimed, "I think it's going to rain!" Another shouted, "It smells like rain is coming soon!" and another, "Do we have time to play before the rain comes?"

I ran inside and grabbed a battery-operated clock and some stickers. When I came back outside, the children gathered around, curious. We talked about the numbers and hands on the clock, and I explained that together they tell us what time it is. Each child then chose a sticker to put on the numeral he or she thought the clock hands would be pointing to when the rain came.

And with that, everyone dispersed and went about their play.

I set the clock aside, turned on some music, and grabbed umbrellas for the moment when the rain came. After quite some time, it finally happened.

Drip.

A chorus of cheers quickly followed the first splash of rain, and we all ran to the clock to see whose stickers the clock hands were pointing to.

Before too much time had passed, a child noticed the raindrops dotting the cement. "Look, Denita! It looks like a dot-to-dot!"

And so it went. I grabbed the sidewalk chalk. I opened up the umbrellas, I turned up the music, and we had a blast laughing, singing, and dancing while we drew lines from dot-to-dot!

Following the minds of the children leads to engaged, focused, real activities that are ripe with learning. Prediction (in this case, using the clock to predict when the rain would start), assessing the accuracy of the prediction (looking at the clock to see where the hands were pointing when the rain started), and observing changes in state of being (watching the pavement change color as it became wet) are key elements of the scientific method. Besides exploring these, the children were using their imaginations, practicing social skills, exercising large- and small-muscle groups, refining hand-eye coordination, gaining better understanding of color, and experiencing the physical world—all because their caregiver reacted in the moment with a learning mind-set that followed the children's lead.

The key to being a good reactive planner is seeing the always-present potential for learning around you. This means seeing the world with a child's fresh eyes as well as your own experience and knowledge so that you can catch learning moments and make the most of them. It means noticing what the children are already learning from their own drive to notice and investigate. It won't take many of these magical moments for you to realize the best learning happens unexpectedly, when the children are leading.

Think of a moment when your reaction to an unexpected incident brought about a fun experience or a valuable piece of learning.

_____

_____

_____

What do you see as your biggest roadblock to becoming a reactive planner?

_____

_____

_____

BE PROACTIVE

In your work as an early learning experience architect, it helps to be proactive about being reactive. Confused? You're not alone—our editor had to take a second look too. Here's what we mean: be prepared for those possible child-led moments you don't yet know are coming. For example, it's springtime. What possible discoveries might children make in spring? With the exception of the occasional pumpkin-obsessed child, pumpkins will not be of interest to young children in spring. Pumpkins just aren't a part of their world in springtime. But flowers, baby birds, bird nests, rain, tree buds, warmer weather—yes. Have books, songs, games, and other materials related to children's possible discoveries within quick reach so you can quickly react to their interests. Be proactive so you can react to the potential learning moments that children generate every day.

Denita's story would not have turned out the same if she hadn't been able to find her clock, stickers, umbrellas, radio, and chalk. Imagine this instead: "Sorry, kids, it'd be fun to connect the dots of rain on the cement, but I have no idea where the chalk is." She knew just where to find the right materials to support the children's interests, enabling her to react quickly to their lead.

Here are two tips for being prepared:

- **Organize.** Know where to find books, puppets, art supplies, and other materials that might come in handy. Actually, don't just know where they are, but be able to get to them too. Knowing that they're in the basement in a musty box next to the chest freezer and the old lawn darts game won't do you any good. Chapter 7 offers a long list of items we think are good to have on hand.

- **Anticipate.** Here's an example: if it's fall, what hands-on items should you have at the ready? Think about what things the children might discover or ask questions about in fall. What colors are they going to be seeing outside? What changes in the weather are taking place? How are the animals in your area reacting to the weather changes? The answers to these questions depend a lot on the climate in your region. In northern latitudes, caterpillars, apples, changing leaves, pumpkins, acorns, squirrels, migrating birds, cooler temperatures, and jackets will probably be on the minds of the kids in your care. Anticipate the children's possible interest and proactively prepare to react to them.

From Denita's World

Two-year-old Avery arrived at child care one cold, cold January morning all excited because "Nita! It's slipplerly out!" Her observation sparked a conversation about ice. Luckily enough, I had bags of ice on hand just in case a moment arose when the children's interest shifted to what the world was currently covered in: ice and snow.

We filled some bowls with water tinted with watercolor, poured the ice into plastic containers, and had an engaging time painting ice cubes. Soothing music filled the air along with conversation about the ice itself. The result was incredibly beautiful, and the process was calming for all of us.

One question came up again and again: How did the ice get to be that shape? Let's face it: ice isn't naturally smooth, rectangular, and precisely shaped. In South Dakota, ice usually forms in long conical shapes like icicles, or flat and slippery shapes like cutting boards. It covers sidewalks, roads, and car windows. The kids were extremely curious about how the ice cubes got their shape.

I posed some questions: "What would happen if we filled some balloons with water and put them outside overnight? What shape would the water balloons be in the morning?" Most of the children thought they'd be flat, like a board.

I got out the balloons, which I always have on hand, and some trinkets. We loaded the balloons with tiny treasures—buttons, silk leaves, and so on—and then we filled them up with water and asked some questions: With the water inside them, what shape are the balloons? Where in the water-filled balloons do the trinkets rest? What do the balloons sound and feel like when we tap them? After we had a pretty good discussion about the water-and-trinket-filled balloons, we placed them in bowls and set the bowls outside.

The following morning, the children were excited to tell me that on their way into my home, they touched the balloons, and not only did the balloons feel hard, but they also still looked like blown-up balloons!

Once all the kids had arrived, we brought the frozen balloons into the house. I had no idea what we would do with them—perhaps put a few in bowls of hot water and observe? Then I remembered some small-handled hammers I'd gotten at the Dollar Tree, so I gathered a sheet, some plastic storage containers (to hold the mess), some goggles, and the hammers.

We started by using scissors to cut the balloons away from the ice shapes inside them. Oh, the amazement! The shape of the ice went unchanged, even when the balloon itself was removed!

We passed the very heavy frozen ice shapes around and felt the burning cold, and then we placed them in the mess-containing containers. We put on the goggles and began pounding the ice balls with hammers. There were three balloons, so three kids at a time had the pleasure of crushing their way to the treasures frozen within.

I learned a few things *very* quickly.

- **You cannot contain the mess made by children who are hammering frozen balloons.** Ice chips flew everywhere!

- **Wearing goggles is a very good idea.** (Again, ice chips flew everywhere!)

- **Things will get wet.** Flying ice chips landing atop a sheet-covered carpeted area will still make for a wet carpet.

- **Children love to hammer frozen balloons.** (And again, ice chips will fly everywhere!)

Once all the treasures had been discovered and the ice balloons reduced to pre-syrup snow cone ice, the children asked, "Can we do that again, Nita?"

So we repeated the process! We put treasures into some balloons, filled the balloons with water, explored what the water in the balloons was like, placed the water-filled balloons in bowls, and set them outside.

The next morning, the children once again came in and very excitedly reported on the state of the ice balloons. Having learned a few valuable lessons myself the day before, I got out several large beach towels and covered the flooring, away from the carpet, with them. I placed the frozen balloons directly on the towels. (I skipped trying to use containers to contain the mess.)

The first child to crack a frozen balloon was greeted by a wet surprise! The balloon hadn't frozen all the way through, and out poured a river of water. This created a buzz of excitement about the potential of the remaining balloons. The others produced a much smaller, yet still significant, river of water. We talked about why there was water inside the ice: the weather outside had warmed up by about twenty degrees overnight, and the ice was different.

The experimenting wasn't over. Among other things, we also tried melting the ice chunks with a hair dryer and an electric skillet set on warm. Whew! The point is, because I was prepared, three days packed full of learning across the (un)curriculum transpired. We enhanced our vocabulary, used senses to explore our world, built self-esteem by hammering extremely heavy and strong frozen balloons, cooperated, took turns, counted treasures, sorted ice chunks by size, solved problems, predicted, and applied newly acquired knowledge to answer questions.

Reflect on a moment (or moments) from your life when you wish you had been better prepared.

_____

_____

_____

What three things should you add to your early learning emergency tool kit?

_____

_____

_____

Bubble-Wrapped Kids

Being too proactive can eliminate terrific learning opportunities for young children. Let's look at some examples. Three children want to color, and two spots are left at the table. Do you get another chair so all three can color, or do you step back and observe how the children handle the situation? A child who has been playing house under a table is about to stand up, but she hasn't come all the way out from under the table. Do you rush in and move her, or do you let her bump her head and learn to be aware of her surroundings? Adults spoil a lot of learning when they are too eager to accommodate or prevent less-than-perfect situations. Adults behave like bubble wrap for children, feeling as if they need to protect kids from life's imperfections. One child feels it is his turn to play with a toy, and he rips it out of another child's hands. In comes an adult to save the day for the child who has been wronged. When will that child learn how to stand up for himself? What happens when children get to elementary school? Who is going to bubble-wrap them there? An average day on the playground can produce a handful of conflicts and confrontations for every child. A program full of adults who suffocate produces children who are not able to cope with the world when it doesn't go their way. Step back and let situations happen. Give children the opportunity to handle them.

BE SPONTANEOUS

The mere thought of the word *spontaneous* makes some people shudder. Mix *spontaneous* with a room full of young children, and some of those people will get downright ill. Because they think that unrelenting chaos will happen if they let go of planning and allow spontaneity to reign, some early learning professionals try to plan spontaneity right out of their programs.

Adults become creatures of habit, stuck in well-established neural pathways, but children thrive on spontaneous learning moments, as long as they have a foundation of predictability in their emotional and physical environments. Kids are like kittens and baby chimps: their curiosity and their need to play lead them to moments of spontaneous experience, which in turn leads them to learning.

Spontaneity is fun. Say you're singing "Yankee Doodle." It's an okay song, but add some spontaneity to it, and you've a fantastic learning opportunity. One fine day at Denita's, everyone was loudly singing "Yankee Doodle" when out of the blue Denita said, "What if Yankee Doodle wasn't riding on a pony? What if he was riding a turtle instead? What do you think he'd call his feather then?"

To her surprise and pleasure, the children responded with "Myrtle!", and now this "Yankee Doodle fill-in-the-blank" game has become a favorite, fantastic way to practice rhyming in a nonthreatening, (un)curriculum way. Good old Yankee has ridden tarantulas, alligators, jellyfish, great white sharks, and all sorts of wild and crazy animals.

In Jeff's program, adventures are a great source of spontaneity. Following the children's whims has led them to spur-of-the-moment bus rides, restaurant lunches, farmer's market honey, conversations with strange dogs and strange humans, a funeral for a dead bird in a downtown trash can, dancing in public fountains, missed naps, and lots of learning.

Spontaneity is as educational as it is fun.

We can't simply explain how spontaneous moments happen. Our best advice is to get up on your tippy-toes and gaze over the edge of the curriculum box toward the surrounding learning opportunities. Thinking outside the box creates outrageously fun and powerful learning moments. Let your silliness out, allow your inner child to leave the time-out chair, be Tom Hanks in *Big*. Think like a three-year-old—then use your access to glue, and paint, and transportation, and other adult-controlled tools to make fun stuff happen.

A bonus to spontaneity is that children love to see adults having fun, laughing, and being silly. It builds bonds and deepens relationships, strengthening your emotional environment.

Some people might argue that children need to learn to control their spontaneity, follow directions, and stay on task in preparation for formal schooling. To that, we inhale deeply, stick out our tongues, put our thumbs in our ears, wiggle our fingers, and exhale with a loud, "Thubpthubpthubpthubpthubpthubpthubpthubpthubpthubpthubpthubp!" There's plenty of time to learn those things when they get to school. Spontaneity is to childhood what whipped cream is to . . . Oh, look, another butterfly!

From Denita's World

Fingernails on chalkboards bother some people, squeaky Styrofoam bothers others, and piles of chalk dust bother me. I can't explain it. They just bother me. My child care children love to make piles of chalk dust then pinch up the chalk and rub it on their hands. It drives me nuts. (Hey, we all have our things-that-send-shivers.) But I realized that making piles of chalk dust was what children wanted to do with the chalk, and it wasn't hurting a thing, of course—just giving me goose bumps is all. Then one hot summer morning, I had a spontaneous moment.

I grabbed paintbrushes and a plastic bucket, filled the bucket with water, and set it down on the cement with the paintbrushes. I patiently waited for the dust piles to appear and to see what the children would do with the supplies. Quickly my eager mess cravers took over. Sure, creativity was involved, but really, folks, for Ella, Avery, and a few others, the mess was the thing. The horrid dust piles they made were quickly transformed into chalk paint, which they used to paint sidewalk, rocks, legs, feet, and hands. Of course my "Oh dear, should they be doing that?" alarm went off, but I quickly shushed it with a sensible, "It's *chalk*. It washes right off, for Pete's sake!"

The children's inquisitive nature took over. Their curiosity pushed this simple, spontaneous moment to great heights. A few of them discovered they could use their hands and feet, plus wet chalk, to make prints. A few more dipped the chalk directly into the water. The pictures they made were beautiful because the wet chalk produced such vibrant colors.

I watched the children and pondered how I could preserve their drawings; simply taking a photo would not do. As I continued to watch them, I wondered if paper towels would pick up their pictures. So I grabbed some, and we laid one sheet over a wet chalk drawing, pressed it down, and lifted up. There, on the paper towel, was the same beautiful picture that had been drawn on the cement. I was just as excited as the children.

Spontaneity got us pretty far that day: first, turning chalk dust to paint; second, using that paint to make handprints, footprints, and tire prints; and third, duplicating the prints on paper towels. What an amazing, discovery-filled, spontaneous morning we had!

Describe how you felt the last time you acted spontaneously.

_____

_____

_____

Spontaneously write down something you've wanted to try in your program, and then make plans to do it as soon as possible.

_____

_____

_____

Young Brains Are Kittens

As we (un)plan for early learning, it is important to remember that the busy brains of small children have a lot in common with cute little kitty cats:

- They need to play.

- They require lots of attention.

- Their interests and focus can change quickly.

- It's hard to keep a bunch of them focused on a single task.

- They like to sink their claws into some things while totally ignoring others—and you can never predict what they'll be interested in.

- They're always on the prowl for stimulation.

- They run on curiosity and are easily distracted by bright shiny objects.

- They need to be kept fed and hydrated.

- They need their sleep.

- They seek challenges and don't always recognize danger . . .

- . . . But they usually land on their feet.

- They are quick and agile, flexible and bendy.

BE OBSERVANT

In an (un)curriculum, your role is to be an observer. There are two ways to be an observer. The first is to step back and be quiet. The second is to be insightful.

The Quiet Observer

Being a quiet observer means resisting the temptation to solve every problem the children encounter. It means not letting your well-established processes ruin the far more fantastic inclinations of a child's unfenced mind. It means not showing children the answers. It means removing yourself and letting their minds do the analyzing, rationalizing, and problem solving. It means letting children discover the answers through trial and error.

Children learn far more through trial-and-error experiences than they do when they are simply shown the answers—and they feel a greater sense of accomplishment, because trial-and-error experiences teach young children the value of persistence. In our instant-gratification, no-need-for-patience society, trial-and-error learning—taking the time to find the answers—gets easily lost. But when you observe quietly, the "I did it!"s that follow the children's trial-and-error experiences make the challenge of remaining quiet worth it.

From Denita's World

I struggle with being quiet. Ask anyone who knows me. God gave me a mouth, and it does not go unused. I struggle on almost a daily basis to put my adult ideas aside. Allowing the children to make their own discoveries and take things in an entirely new, unimaginable direction is sometimes a challenge for me. The results are always worth the restraint, though, which makes being quiet increasingly easier for me to do.

Recently my eleven-year-old son, Landon, and I brought home some wonderful cardboard supports from appliance boxes. (You can find your own set of these beauties by asking for them at your local appliance retailer.) They remind me of rain gutters but are made out of unbelievably sturdy cardboard about three and a half feet long. To me it was clear that their true calling was to be ramps. I couldn't wait to see what my group of three-, four-, and five-year-olds would do with them.

I plopped the supports on the floor and waited for the children to arrive the next morning. Once they did, the very first thing they did with the ramps was to measure, to my complete surprise! They compared themselves to the height of the ramps. They laid the ramps on the floor and tried to guess what animals would be the same size. The kids led themselves through a lesson on measurement that was at least twenty minutes long. They compared and contrasted, using scientific words such as *longer, shorter, bigger,* and *smaller,* and worked together.

Eventually the moment I had anticipated did arrive, but not exactly as I'd expected.

Jack, holding a ramp and comparing himself to it, exclaimed, "Nita! I'm the same size as this one!" Ty was quick to object. "No, you aren't, Jack! You're holding it like a slide! Hold it straight and you are smaller." Sure enough, Ty was right. But at that point, it didn't really matter, because the word *slide* had entered the exploration, and the rest was history. The ramps finally became ramps and slides. Once in a while they're other things—supports for a playhouse, balance beams, and surf boards—but for the most part, they've settled comfortably into the role I'd assumed they would. But had I interrupted the children's exploration to show them what to do with these cardboard supports, the lesson in measurement never would have happened.

I continued my role as silent observer while the children built the ramps, even though it was obvious to me that they were too steep and the balls would bounce right out of them. I bit my tongue as the children built ramps with corner turns that lacked any joints to help the balls change direction. I was proud of myself. I stepped back, I observed, and the children did their own work. The ramps they built and the trial-and-error process they experienced were priceless learning. My messing with them would have ruined it.

The Insightful Observer

It takes a very knowledgeable and receptive person to be an insightful observer: knowledgeable in the ways of young children and receptive to the learning in their play. Your role as an insightful observer is very important; it takes an insightful observer to educate people who think overly planned, structured, fenced-in learning is how young children are wired to learn.

Most people aren't able to break down play to see what learning is really going on. For example, they can't see that climbing up slides is a stage of prewriting, because children need to have strong and coordinated large muscles before they can gain control over the small ones. They don't understand that basic skills like sorting and patterning are needed for children to do more complex things like counting, writing, recognizing letters, reading, and getting along with other people. It's the job of an insightful observer to be knowledgeable about the basic skills children need to acquire before they can achieve the more obvious academic skills, receptive to the ways that children hone skills through play, and able to express all of this to parents and other adults so they understand the power of play.

Denita has been a group fitness instructor for seventeen years. When she teaches a class involving choreography, she can't just throw a sixty-four count routine at her class. She has to break down sixty-four counts into smaller parts to create a manageable, teachable, and learnable routine. First, she has to teach an eight-count move, and then another. Then she combines those to create a sixteen-count miniroutine. The class does the miniroutine again and again to ensure that everyone knows it. Then Denita teaches a second sixteen-count segment that she later blends seamlessly with the first one. Finally, she repeats the resulting thirty-two-count routine to create the entire complex sixty-four-count routine, and now the class can easily achieve the whole of it.

This is the same process caregivers must go through to help children learn complex, sixty-four-count academic skills like reading. For example, consider letter recognition. Do you begin with letters? No. The very first skill children need to recognize letters is spatial awareness. They must become aware of their body and objects in space—where they are in relation to other objects; where up is; where down is. They need to recognize that if asked what color shoes a friend is wearing, they should aim their eyes down to where the feet are, not up to where the heads are. Children need to be aware of differences and similarities. They need to know order and sequencing—what comes first, what comes second. They need an understanding of *over, under, beside, next,* and *between.* All of these concepts need to be learned before children can possibly distinguish one letter from another.

How do children acquire this degree of understanding? *Through play.* This is why play is more effective at preparing them for academics than worksheets or flash cards. Children do not develop spatial awareness through flash cards, but they do develop spatial awareness through running, climbing up the slide, building with blocks, pouring water, moving sand, and a hundred other forms of play.

As an insightful observer, you need to understand the background of every academic skill in this way so you can show parents and other adults how children learn through play. You need to be able to help them understand that playing for hours prepares children for academics more effectively than learning flash cards.

From Denita's World

Kindergarten assessment makes me crabby, plain and simple. I despise kindergarten assessment. I think it is a very inaccurate reading of a child's abilities. So when one of my child care dads was picking up his child and started the following conversation, I almost ran inside to grab my crabby hat.

Brian: Well, you didn't do as good of a job with this one as you did with the first.

Me: Huh?

Brian: Oh, we had kindergarten assessment last night.

Me: Oh Brian . . . Don't even get me started on kindergarten assessment.

[Pause]

Me again: Look, you just can't compare children. Your girls are each their own person. Anastacia wanted to learn more and more; she would ask me how to spell words, how to make letters and numbers. She would play "Nita" and teach the other kids. Avery is just loving her imagination and playing. She is the most imaginative little girl I know, and that alone is a grand quality. When she's ready for more, she'll let us know. I have every ounce of confidence in her ability to lead her own learning.

Brian: Hey, I was just joking with you. (Brian and his wife are good, good friends of ours.)

Me: I know. But I despise kindergarten assessment. They take the kids into a strange room with a strange person and ask them questions. Any child with a tinge of stubbornness can see through this act and refuses to show what she knows. I guarantee that's what Avery did. Okay, so what did they say? What does she *not* know?

Brian (a bit scared of me by this point): Really, Denita, I was just joking. We aren't worried, but if you want to know, they said she can't rhyme.

Me (outraged): What? The heck she can't rhyme! Whenever we read rhyming stories, I leave out the rhyming word and let the kids fill it in. We were just reading *The Tickle Monster*, and the line was something like, "And now my fine kitties, it's time to tickle your . . .," and Avery shot to her feet and enthusiastically yelled out, "Titties!" She most certainly can rhyme.

After a lot of laughing, I told Brian not to be concerned about the fact that she said "titties." When I teach rhyming, anything goes. If I ask what rhymes with *cat*, the room is filled with silly words all at once—*rat, tat, gat, hat, zat, dat*. The key component to rhyming is the end sound, and the sillier and more nonsensical the word, the more the focus is on the key sound. (This is my own opinion, but I know it to be true.)

This was a simple five-minute conversation that led to some good laughs, good educating, and an appreciation for what Avery could do. Avery did go to kindergarten, and she did very well. That summer, before the start of kindergarten, she started asking me how to spell words. She started carrying the clipboard and pens around so that she could write words and then read them to me. I pointed out these milestones to Brian and Christine to help them feel confident that, yes, Avery could be trusted with her own learning.

BE FLEXIBLE

We're not asking you to put your left ankle behind your head and touch your right ankle to your left elbow (pause for a moment and paint that mental picture). That kind of flexibility is great, but we're more interested in seeing you create some flexibility in your schedule and your mind-set when you plan for early learning.

Too much rigidity and control hinder your ability to design fresh and engaging early learning experiences. For example, it's hard to spontaneously devote as much time as the kids need to the giant black cricket they just discovered in the sandbox when you hate bugs and lunch starts in exactly—*exactly*—six minutes. It's also difficult to explore all the wonders of mud if your mind-set is antimess and antisquishy. Being flexible means being able to drop an activity you thought would be fun and following the children's lead instead. It also means not allowing your personal dislikes, hang-ups, and expectations to hold kids back from learning opportunities. Your dislike of bugs should not keep kids from learning about bugs.

Get comfortable with flexibility. Looking at your watch, thinking, "Gosh, if we keep looking for caterpillars, we'll never have time for the craft that came in the curriculum box, and I paid good money for that—I don't want to waste it," is not a good way to spend caterpillar time.

From Denita's World

To be completely honest, I am not the most flexible person in the world—in every sense of the word. There are times when I really let loose and start fixing lunch at 11:45 instead of 11:30, but for the most part, I am a creature of habit, and, quite frankly, by 11:30 I'm dreaming of the break that naptime sometimes brings me. But naptime can't happen until lunchtime is over. Flexibility doesn't stop with scheduling or planning. You're being flexible anytime you let a child's idea override your preconceived plan. This requires giving up control and trusting the children as learners. Doing this does not have to be a big complex thing, either. Sometimes all you have to do is fade into the background.

I was quite proud of the flexibility I demonstrated one bright sunny day when a group of my girls requested the chalk. I quickly ran into the garage to grab the bucket and spied my dollar store cheese graters, which I'd thought were long gone! I grabbed them happily along with a bucket for water and some card stock that I'd already cut into five-by-eight-inch pieces.

As I walked across the yard, a small crowd of kids formed. I'd nabbed their curiosity with the cheese graters. When I went to the hose and turned on the water, I *really* grabbed their attention.

I set down the stuff and demonstrated the right way (*my* way) to use the materials: using the cheese grater, carefully grate the big pieces of chalk into the water. I pointed out the fact that the grated chalk floated atop the water. After grating several different colors of chalk, I took a piece of card stock and laid it on top of the water and watched it float too. I picked up the card stock quickly and flipped it over to reveal a beautiful spattering of color. There were "oohs" and "ahs," and everyone was eager to try.

Here's where I stretched, becoming more flexible by stepping into the background: I left the materials and walked away. It was hard but had to be done. I wanted to be in control, and I wanted the children to love my activity, but instead I stretched—I became flexible so they could play, explore, and discover. I let go of center stage and faded into the scenery. And so much more learning occurred than would have had I stayed on center stage to push my own vision.

Here is just some of the learning that happened when I stepped back:

- **The children cooperated.** Three of the kids argued over who should go first and why but came up with a solution surprisingly quickly. They restored the peace, and no one shed a single tear. If I hadn't faded into the background, then I would have solved the argument by deciding who would go first, second, and third, and the children would not have had a chance to work it out on their own.

- **The children experimented.** The first child had a hard time getting the chalk flecks to float because she was holding the grater too far away from the water. I knew that the chalk would float only if it landed gently on the water, but I didn't say so. After some experimentation, she solved the problem herself and eagerly shared her discovery with the other children.

- **The children discovered.** Another child decided not to waste the chalk bits floating to the bottom of the water. She pushed the card stock to the bottom, swirling it around a bit. When she pulled it from the water, all those beautiful specks of colorful chalk had created a lovely shade of brown. I cringed when I saw this, thinking, *Oh, good grief, that's* not *what they're supposed to be doing!* But I kept my thoughts to myself and watched as this brand-new technique took over.

- **The children discovered some more.** A pair of two-year-olds snuck behind the older kids and dropped some chalk sticks into their bucket of water. The big kids yelled until one realized how awesome it was to draw with wet chalk. It was almost like painting. From this accidental discovery, even more beautiful pictures were made. If I hadn't faded into the background, then this discovery wouldn't have happened.

Much more learning occurred when I gave up center stage and let the children explore the materials. Sticking with my own plan offered only one way of doing things, but ideas and learning blossomed when I faded into the scenery. We still had lunch on time that day, everyone napped, and I took my break at the right time—even though I was flexible!

What do you think about your own flexibility? Could you be more flexible in some areas? Are you already pretty flexible? What internal feelings or external forces get in the way of being more flexible?

_____

_____

What one thing could you change to make your program's schedule a little more flexible?

_____

_____

BE RELAXED

If you can relax and follow the children's lead, we guarantee learning will occur—good, solid, memorable learning.

Sounds simple, but we're sure you know it's not.

Most caregivers find it incredibly difficult to relax. After all, there are noses to be wiped, papers to be worked, errands to be run, and stern looks to be given. There are worries to be worried, mental lists to be checked, snacks to be served, and diapers to be changed. And there's always a thought, a responsibility, or a memory pulling you away from the *right now*.

Hard as it is, relaxing and being right here, right now are the best things caregivers can do for the children in their care and for themselves. A relaxed adult means relaxed children. Children who are relaxed are more focused and willing to explore the world, which means they learn more and retain their learning better. Relaxing helps build strong emotional environments. Relaxing makes you better at all the other things we've suggested in this chapter. When you relax, you see more clearly, react more appropriately, and tune in to your environment better. Relaxing also slows you down so you enjoy things more.

Don't worry about parents' expectations. Relax and let the children lead you. Have confidence in the abilities of the children to take charge of their own learning and involve you only when they need you. Don't force children to learn. Relax and let them show you signs that they're ready for more. (That's where being a good observer comes in handy!)

From Denita's World

I was thirty-nine and had never played with natural clay. I'd never touched its silky smoothness or used more muscles than I knew I had just to manipulate it a bit. It was love at first touch!

I'd come across a heavy box of natural clay at the craft store. My own children (ages eleven and twelve) had an awesome time playing with the clay, and I realized the child care kids would really love it too. I had no idea what exactly they would do with it but knew it was worth the mess to find out.

The next Monday, I set out a bucket full of warm water and then

placed a large sensory tub on the picnic table and clunked a glob of clay into it. A curious audience of children assembled. Next, I took some plastic lacing, held it like dental floss, and cut the clay into a few big chunks. I dumped in about thirty sea-creature beads, poured a little water in the tub, and stepped back.

Throughout the process of setting up, questions flew: "What is that?" "Are we gonna get to play in it?" "What does it do?" My answers were "natural clay," "yep," and "I don't know—why don't you tell me?" With that, I relaxed and stepped away, feeling confident they would find some amazing things to do with the clay.

The children were instantly impressed by how smooth the clay felt, and soon they'd created slides for the fish beads to slide down, a turtle island on which the turtle beads could sun themselves, and a nest that quickly became home to dolphin beads. The kids covered their hands in clay, making "monster hands."

The play continued, and the mess grew. Eventually we added vinegar and baking soda and liquid watercolor—clay, water, beads, and colored lava were everywhere! I felt a bit stressed by it all, but I took a few deep breaths, relaxed, and went with the flow.

It's often our inclination to get tensed up about messes, but the children can sense our tension, and it holds them back. The clay experience wouldn't have been as successful if I'd interrupted the action with a tight jaw and worried look. By stepping back and relaxing, I helped the kids relax, go with the flow, and play. The only plan I'd made for the morning was the plopping of clay; I put the rest of the learning in the hands of the children.

Try this now and whenever you're feeling rushed:

- Sit comfortably with your eyes closed.

- Breathe slowly—in through your nose and out through your mouth.

- When distracting thoughts pop into your head, acknowledge them and then blow them away with your next exhalation.

- Feel your muscles relax, your pulse slow, and your stress melt away.

- After a few minutes, open your eyes and return to your day.

(Un)planning can be scary and overwhelming if for your whole career you've been told to plan, plan, plan. But in our experience, the ideas outlined above lead to deep and learning-rich play. Remember that (un)planning does not mean kicking back with an umbrella drink and allowing chaos to reign. It means becoming more proactive, spontaneous, flexible, observant, and relaxed.

Making the transition from a planning mind-set to an (un)planning mind-set will take some doing, especially if you've been a ridgid planner for as long as you can remember. The effort is worth it, though. The children in your care will learn more and be more engaged because the experiences you help them create are more connected to their own interests. Give (un)planning a try, but don't rush into it. Make small changes over time—baby steps—which happens to be the topic of the next chapter.

Taking Baby Steps

Those who expect moments of change to be comfortable and free of conflict have not learned their history.
> —Joan Wallach Scott, "History in Crisis? The Others' Side of the Story"

After you've done a thing the same way for two years, look it over carefully. After five years, look at it with suspicion. And after ten years, throw it away and start all over.
> —Alfred Edward Perlman

Making program changes can be overwhelming, and taking on too many changes all at once can have disastrous effects. Take baby steps. Making little changes over time allows you to be more thoughtful and creates better choices. Incremental change results in less caregiver stress, because small changes over time are easier to adjust to.

In this chapter, we give you two methods for transforming your program. The first is Denita's story, which will tell you about the steps she took to make changes in her own family child care program. The second is a tried-and-true way of experimenting that will help you shake things up a little—just once, or over and over again, if you choose.

Read Denita's story. Experiment and shake things up. Stick your toe in the water. We dare you!

Denita's Story

I've always loved a weekend when nothing's been planned and options are endless and open to any spontaneous whim. If it's gorgeous outside, I can take a nice long bike ride and then head to the pool with my family. If it's cold and yucky, perhaps I'll stay indoors for a lazy morning of lounging followed by an afternoon matinee. Why, then, was I so hooked on planning out the children's time during the week? Why couldn't I see that, like me, they also became tired of structure and enjoyed spontaneous whimsy?

Structure is what I learned through my own formal education: children need structure. They need a sense of order. They feel safe when life is predictable. Structure can offer predictability. But I took those facts to the extreme. I put structure everywhere! Heck, I even gave structure to circle time! First we sang the welcome song, and then the weather wizard did his thing, and then we sang a weather song, and then we did the calendar, and then, then, then. Circle time was the same every single day. I even printed up its order to hand out to the parents! In fact, I was so consistent with the structure of circle time that the children began to rely on it, and if something about it changed, I had behavior problems on my hands. Some children would freak out if we did the calendar before the weather. Let's be honest: that's not something to freak out about.

I called my program child-centered and child-led, because I knew that the children liked to do what I planned for them. Now I know that putting my plans at the center, no matter how much the children like them, is not what child-centered means.

Making the change from a very structured program to a truly child-centered, child-led (un)curriculum was not quick for me. In fact, I've been transitioning toward it for over eight years. I started by making one small change, then another, and then another. Now I hope that you can find a way to move away from adult-centered structure to a truly child-centered, child-led (un)curriculum, one that will work for you and the children in your program.

Here are the five steps I went through as I moved toward an (un)curriculum:

1. I added flexibility.

2. I messed it up.

3. I accidentally (un)planned.

4. I adopted Monday Discovery Day.

5. I planned a plop.

I didn't foresee these five steps, but looking back, I can now see that they're how the process evolved. It was gradual, and it worked for me and for the children in my program. Feel free to take what I've learned and apply it to your program in a way that works for you and your children. You can simply read through what follows for ideas, or you can use the five steps as a template for planning your own gradual change to an (un)curriculum.

STEP ONE: ADD FLEXIBILITY

The first change I made was to add flexibility to my program. And I mean, I *really* added flexibility.

You may be thinking, "Oh, I'm already flexible." Are you really,

though? I thought I was flexible. I thought I had always supported "teachable moments." Then the children discovered a caterpillar during my unit on the senses (see chapter 6 for the whole caterpillar story), and my reaction to their discovery is what made me realize I wasn't as flexible as I thought.

Really being flexible means really listening to the kids. It means not imposing the plan but setting it aside for a while, or, possibly—*gasp!*—forever. It means doing what the children are interested in the very moment they're interested in it. I wanted to be consistently flexible.

I found adding flexibility was a very small step, one I could accomplish reasonably and one that did not rock the boat much at all. I added flexibility, but I continued with my planning as usual. I planned out September through May, including letters, numbers, shapes, and colors. But instead of using a pen to do my planning, I planned it all out in pencil so I could easily erase and rearrange at the hint of a new discovery by the children.

Interestingly enough, the first benefits I enjoyed from being flexible were fewer discipline issues and less frustration. When children are forced to do something they don't want to do, they rebel, and if they aren't enjoying something, they pick on other children and get restless. I felt less frustrated because I no longer had the we-need-to-get-this-done-and-every-child-needs-to do-it feeling. If a child didn't want to paint that day, that was fine; it was her choice. When I sensed the children were more interested in a caterpillar than in smelling with their noses, I let that interest change the direction of our week. Making young children do what you want them to do does not work nearly as well as following their lead.

STEP TWO: MESS IT UP

My second step toward an (un)curriculum was to mess it all up. Structure offers many benefits to children—but (un)structure holds even more. (Un)structure offers true, open, engaging, and meaningful learning to children.

When I messed it all up, I stopped breaking the days into small segments of time: no more circle time, group activity time, sharing time, or station time. Instead, we experienced those learning opportunities as we fancied, and the days' structure came in the form of a consistent daily flow—hugs and a warm welcome upon the children's arrival every day, breakfast soon thereafter, and after breakfast, play. The children knew that when they played after breakfast, they might be playing by themselves, with one friend, or with a group; in an organized activity, reading books, inside, outside, or both, singing songs, exploring, getting messy, cleaning up, and cooperating; and just about everything else imaginable.

After play came lunch, and after lunch came cozy-blanket rest and book after book. Following nap was more playtime, then snack, and then it was time to go home. I learned that structure did not have to mean every single moment of the day was planned out and predictable, but that a general, consistent flow gave the children enough of the sense of security they needed. In addition, the lack of a traditional segmented structure handed control of the day over to the children, empowering them as capable learners.

Planning

Even though I messed it up, I still got to do my planning. I still planned for all of the typical components of the day—circle time, group time, station time, and so on—but I got rid of the time limits and the order of events. If stations lasted until it was time for lunch, then the group activity I thought we'd do would just wait until the next day.

What I changed about my planning was the format. Before I began messing it up, I planned by theme. I decided how long we would do the theme according to how many activities and projects there were in it. I then planned out each day. I planned each circle time, each group activity time, every station. The problem was, of course, that this method of planning reflected nothing of the children's interest levels.

My new messed-up format was simple: I listed all of the possible things we could do to learn about a particular theme, and that was it. I chose a letter that would go along with the theme and different ways we could learn more and more about that letter. For example, for October, I planned Spiders, Pumpkins, Owls, Monsters, and Halloween

(letters *S*, *P*, *O*, *M*, and *H*). I wanted to accomplish all of these themes in October. Under each theme, I listed all the possible songs, books, art explorations, science discoveries, stations, and social experiences I could conceive of. The children and I would then explore the theme, moving on to the next item in the list as their interest in one activity died. When we'd exhausted the theme, we'd move on to the next one. In this style of planning, my need for a sense of control was met because I knew what we could possibly do, and I was prepared for it. I had the activity materials handy and was ready to run at a moment's notice. But I also was able to give the children more control, and they were able to lead me a little bit more. I simply had to be alert to their signals and responsive to their needs. Messing it up allowed me to be way more flexible and provided room for the spontaneity I now appreciate.

There are so many benefits to this messing-it-up style of planning. The one that stands out the most to me is that it's less stressful—less stress on me and less stress on the children. I can't tell you how many art processes I've rushed in my thirteen years of family child care simply because we were racing against the clock. A rushed child is not a happy one, and if I'm stressed, I guarantee that my stress rubs off on the kids. Getting rid of the schedule and opening up each day to children's interests was one of the best things I ever did.

Circle

Circle time stuck. The kids continued to gravitate toward their circle spots after picking up the toys, even after I'd removed their names from the floor. But what we did during circle time changed. It became more of a motivate 'em time, which was good. It also became a time to invoke a sense of inquiry. I used all sorts of tricks to inspire imaginations and interest in what I'd planned. I was successful most of the time, and when I wasn't, I simply followed the children where they were leading me.

We no longer did calendar time, and not a single child asked where the calendar had gone. Let's face the cold, hard truth: teaching the days of the week with a graph of squares isn't the most effective way to learn about days and weeks. It's not fun, and it's not very meaningful. We continued to refer to the days of the week and to talk about yesterday, today, and tomorrow, but instead of looking to a square, we did something concrete each day to make that day special and different from the others.

Every Friday we had pizza. Each Monday stood out because we hadn't seen each other for three sleeps.

I encourage you to mess it up a bit. Keep your plan, but open your days to the possibilities. I really think you'll enjoy the benefits immediately.

STEP THREE: ACCIDENTALLY (UN)PLAN

After taking the second step of messing it up, I didn't make any drastic changes for several years. I carefully honed my ability to really listen to and follow the children. I found a happy place that incorporated my plans and their interests. Messing it up really worked well for me, and I was getting better than ever at being flexible and setting my plans aside when need be. I also learned to plan only a few months at a time instead of nine months at once. I could add personal touches to the plans this way and make our learning even more meaningful.

Step three, accidental (un)planning, came about out of my own sheer laziness and, as the step suggests, completely by accident. Because I was still planning a few months at a time, I needed to find time in my own schedule more often to do that planning. Eventually I found myself facing a planless Monday morning because I'd used my planning time to do something else. I had no plans as the next week approached. So I decided to try (un)planning, which I guess just means letting go and trusting that the children will provide a path to follow every day. On that first planless Monday, I just sat back, held my breath, and prayed. Fortunately, Brady arrived excited to announce that there was a bird nest in his front yard. His house was about five blocks away, a walkable distance, so we headed out on a walk to share in the joy of Brady's new discovery.

We came back from our walk full of questions about birds and their nests: How do birds make nests? What do they make them with? Why do they make them in a tree? I quickly dug out my bird books. (I keep my books organized alphabetically by title, and then catalog them all in a binder according to theme, so thank goodness, I could quickly find what I needed.) After learning a lot of facts about birds, I rooted around in my craft supply closet and found a couple of bags of colorful feathers. The children spent the next half hour blowing feathers around the room and catching them, first with their hands, then with their fingers, elbows, tummies, even noses! We talked about how easy it was to make a feather fly with just a simple puff of air, and we compared feathers to other objects to see if a puff of air had the same effect on them. The children verbalized what they were learning as they were learning it. It was spontaneous, child-led learning at its finest.

When we settled down for a story, we read *The Perfect Nest* by Catherine Friend—a hilarious tale about a cat who builds a perfect nest to attract the perfect chicken to lay a perfect egg for Jack, the cat, to make into a delicious omelet. After we finished the book, we continued our discussion about nests, and we wondered what a perfect nest would look like. After a lot of imagining, we decided to build our own perfect nest, complete with every couch cushion and pillow and blanket in my house.

Later, while fixing lunch, I reviewed the morning in my head. Wow! I'd done it! I'd gone completely (un)planned, and I'd survived! I'd managed to let go, even if by accident, and the children led me. They had taken over their own learning, and I don't think I could have planned such a fantastic morning. I might have been able to plan something similar, but it wouldn't have been as honest or uninhibited; undoubtedly there would have been a whiff of my agenda underlying it. And even though I'd become quite good at messing it up, I bet I would have rushed the children a little, if only for my own excitement in seeing their responses to the next planned activity. At this point in my transition, I'd developed a great deal of respect for flexibility and spontaneous learning. (Un)planning happened more and more frequently as I slowly gave the control to the children and more and more comfortably followed their lead. Stepping back and seeing how much rich learning takes place in (un)planned moments was a real eye opener for me. Next time you see an opportunity to (un)plan some learning, please take it—it'll be worth the effort.

STEP FOUR: ADOPT MONDAY DISCOVERY DAY

It took about four years from that first accidentally (un)planned Monday—the day of Brady's bird nest discovery—for me to make Monday Discovery Day official. Now, every single Monday I sit back and just wait to see where the children lead me. It has become a planned day of (un)planning. The thing is, those of us who really love to plan and organize often need help letting go. My Monday Discovery Days have become a planned day of letting go—and the results have been fantastic!

Here's an example of a pretty typical Monday Discovery Day. One Monday, the kids realized that Valentine's Day was quickly approaching, so they got busy cutting out hearts, their conversations about Valentine's Day filling the room. After some time, they asked me to get my guitar out so we could sing. We quickly picked up the scissors and paper and sat in our circle spots (some habits never die—letting go is hard). I took a few requests, and we did a little singing, but the topic of Valentine's Day kept coming up. To build on their interest in the holiday, I decided to set my guitar aside and said to the children, "If we're all so interested in Valentine's Day, then let's talk about what letter we should celebrate this week." They gave their answer quickly: *V*!

"Valentine starts with *V*, Nita!"

"Yes, it does. Hold on, though. Let me grab a marker and the easel."

The word list we created for *V* was not long. It held just three words—*valentine*, *Valentine's Day*, and *Velcro*—which told me that the letter *V* wasn't very important to them and that it probably shouldn't be given an entire week's attention.

I said, "Hmm, wow, *V* isn't a very exciting letter, is it, guys? It's kind of boring, huh? Are there any other boring letters? Should we have a boring letter week instead of just a *V* letter week, and get them all out of the way?"

That's what we did. We celebrated *V*, *W*, *U*, and *X* that week and learned more about Valentine's Day too. We did experiments with Water, played with Velcro, colored Upside down and Under tables, and played the Xylophone.

This scheduled day of letting go and seeing where the kids will take me has helped me continue to give up control and trust them to lead their own learning. I've also learned that stepping back—even just a bit—has helped the kids grow as thinkers and leaders. They see that I value their opinions, ideas, and choices.

Building time into your weekly schedule in which you commit yourself to giving up control and letting the kids lead will help you move into an (un)curriculum. It will take some time, but the payoffs are worth the effort.

STEP FIVE: PLAN A PLOP

The most recent step I've added to my own journey from lesson-plan-book lover to (un)curriculum facilitator is Step Five: Plan a Plop. The concept of plopping is a relatively new one for me, and it's grown out of my experiences with (un)planning and Monday Discovery Day.

When you plan a plop, you simply introduce something new into your environment—you just plop it out there and see what happens. (Un)plan a book, a song, a messy mud or paint or cooking opportunity, a strange new item (maybe a Dumpster-dive find), or whatever, and just plop it. Put the object out there, and then step back and be quiet and insightful. You can go ahead and have a guess at the direction you *think* the children might take the plopped object so you can support their explorations, but oh—the extraordinary ideas the children come up with will astound you! Once you plop the object, be ready to simply follow the children's lead. Expect the unexpected.

A few weeks ago, I plopped *The Ice Cream King* by Steve Metzger and Julie Downing. It's a delicious, imaginative read involving an entire kingdom made of ice cream. The words are as delicious as the illustrations, and it can make the most reserved imagination seem wild! Even so, I never thought plopping it would open up the vast, wonderful learning opportunities it did.

I found *The Ice Cream King* at the local bookstore and gave it a read. Then, at Target, I stumbled upon some vanilla-scented lip balm. Next to it was chocolate-scented lip balm, and below it, banana split–scented lip balm. The gears in my head immediately began to turn, and a new scentful idea was born.

The next day, I plopped the book. The children asked me to read it aloud again and again. When the "Read it again!"s subsided, I picked up and shook the drawstring bag I'd tossed the scented lip balms into. The children's eyes filled with wonder as they tried to guess what might be inside it.

I opened the bag and picked out the vanilla- and the chocolate-scented lip balms and then called up the first child. "Hello, ma'am. Would you like chocolate or vanilla ice cream today?"

The child responded excitedly, "Vanilla, please."

I asked for her hand and then rubbed some of the vanilla lip balm to the back of it. Then I said, "Now reach into the bag and choose a surprise topping for your ice cream." Inside were even more scented lip balms: banana split, very berry, and peppermint.

Once all of the children were finished sniffing their ice cream treats, they began pretending the ice cream was melting and encouraged each other to eat it quickly and to be careful not to spill it. From there, a few weeks' worth of imaginative ice cream play ensued. First came baby oil and flour ice cream, which led to ice cream treat creations using PVC pipe and sliced pool noodles. One ice cream creation seemed to stretch into

another until finally the children were begging for the real thing. They wanted to make their own real ice cream treats and gobble them up!

Eventually I surprised the children with all the ice cream toppings they could possibly want to put on their choice of vanilla or chocolate ice cream. The children were in charge. Their bodies literally shook, they were working so hard scooping the ice cream. They sliced their own bananas and squeezed their own chocolate syrup. Their favorite part was squooshing their own whipped topping out of the can.

All of this fun and learning happened because I had plopped a book about ice cream, found some scented lip balm to spark imaginations, and stepped back to let creativity run wild.

I've affectionately named another good plop the Great Box Experiment of 2010. I asked all of my child care families to collect and bring in boxes over the course of a month. The boxes, I told them, would replace all of the toys in my program. I'd leave out only the kitchen set, the balls, the cars, and the dollhouse people. Everything else I'd put in the closet.

On the first day of the Great Box Experiment of 2010, I'd gathered roughly seventy-five boxes. I taped some together using lots of duct tape, and I created trifold panels, though I never once referred to them as panels. Nope, they were ski-jump ramps, ball ramps, car ramps, sandy beaches, bridges, fort walls, tunnels, and rivers. I cut down a few other boxes, and some of the children opened them up and imagined them

into minivans large enough to supply three children transportation to run errands at once.

A few days into the box experiment, I plopped the book *Not a Box* by Antoinette Portis, which spurred their imaginations even more.

After I plopped the boxes that first day, I stepped out of the way. It was a great time for me to be a quiet and insightful observer. In fact, throughout the entire box experiment, I didn't offer a single suggestion and I didn't solve a single problem. The children worked together like I'd never seen them do before. Their vocabularies were being enhanced, theories of physics explored, large and small muscles working hard, and social skills challenged and polished. More learning came from those boxes than I ever could have planned.

I've plopped plastic dryer ducts, chalk and a bucket of water, shaving cream and squeegees, boxes, Dumpster-dive finds, songs, and books. And did you notice how in both of my plopping examples, I added a second or even a third plop to the plop? (*Plopping* has quickly become one of my favorite words!) Every plop brought different outcomes. All of them inspired great child-led moments when I let them. The key to plopping is to know your children, to have an idea of where a plop might go, and to try to be prepared for possible outcomes.

The journey from a teacher-led curriculum to a truly child-led, child-centered (un)curriculum is full of learning for both you and the children. It's a process that takes time and involves steps whose value cannot be overestimated. Start your own journey today. Follow my steps if you'd like, or let a plop inspire you to take an entirely different path. The important thing to remember is to make small changes that create a seamless transition for you and the children in your program.

Experiment and Shake Things Up

Ready to go? Here's another way you could take the plunge and follow the children's lead—even if just for today. Experiment and shake things up a bit using the three lists that follow. The first one lists everyday objects and supplies; the second, places you are likely to have in your program space; the third details simple actions. We did our best to come up with a lot of interesting objects and supplies, places, and actions, but we also provided room for you to add your own ideas to the lists. If you come up with something really good, drop us an e-mail so we can try it out!

Here's how the experimenting works: just pick an item from each list, put them together, and add children. For example, if Peggy Sue and her best buddy, Becka, have been pinching each other during a spat, you might select "clothespins" from list one, "under the table" from list two, and "share" from list three. Hand the girls a bunch of clothespins, demonstrate how clothespins can become pinching machines, and suggest that the girls go under the kitchen table to play—and *then* nonchalantly remind them to share. There's a chance they'll immediately start pinching each other with the clothespins, but it's more likely that they'll start to

play. They may use the clothespins to secure doll blankets to the table so they can create a fort. They may divide the pins evenly and clip them to their clothing; they may use them to pinch stuffed animals; they may use them as tweezers to pick up other objects; or they may spend an hour repeatedly counting the clips. The "under the table" aspect is important here, too, because it gives these two children who weren't getting along very well some privacy and a chance to spend time together. This bit of seclusion offers them a great opportunity to work on their self-regulation and social skills while exploring the new material. Flexible (un)curriculum moments like these are full of hands-on chances to actually practice skills that more rigid curriculums often just lecture or sing about. Playing under a table with someone you haven't been getting along with teaches social skills much more effectively than a circle time let's-be-friends monologue.

You can also shake things up by selecting more than one item from the first list. For example, on a recent trip to Alabama, Jeff and his wife stopped to play at their friend Kay's family child care program. Just for fun, they brought totes of potting soil and added a can of Crisco to each tote, which resulted in nearly four hours of messy play, including children going head-first down a slide covered in Crisco-mud road blocks and games of catch with Crisco-mud balls that had been rolled in colored rice.

There's really no wrong way to use these lists. They are intended to help spark ideas and connect to children's interests. You simply need to pay attention to the children's interests, connect those to items on these lists, and create a play scenario. After that, all you need to do is step back a bit, let the children lead, and be supportive. These lists could become the foundation of your (un)curriculum and lead to hundreds of thousands of ways to follow the interests of the children. Go ahead and experiment, shake things up, but ease into it. Remember, take baby steps. Never let a combination get too far beyond your comfort zone.

EVERYDAY OBJECTS AND SUPPLIES

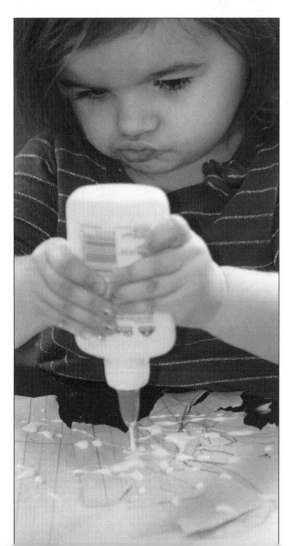

Action figures
Aluminum foil
Baby dolls
Baby oil
Baking soda
Balloons
Bandages
Baster
Bird seed
Boards, wooden
Boulders
Bubble solution
Bubble wrap
Buckets
Cable ties
Cardboard boxes, extra large
Cardboard boxes, large
Cardboard boxes, medium
Cardboard boxes, small
Cardboard tubes, long
Cardboard tubes, short
Cars and trucks
Catalogs
Cement mix
Chopsticks
Cinnamon
Clay
Clothespins
Construction paper
Corks
Corn starch
Cotton balls
Cotton swabs
Craft sticks
Crayons
Cream
Cups
Diapers, clean, cloth
Diapers, fresh, disposable

Dry cereal
Eggs, fresh
Eggs, plastic
Elastic
Envelopes
Eyedropper
Fabric
Flagging tape
Flaxseed
Flour
Flowers
Food coloring
Fun noodles (pool
  noodles)
Garlic powder
Glitter
Glue
Grass clippings
Gravel
Ice, cubes
Ice, large block
Index cards
Kitchen tongs
Leaves, dry
Leaves, green
Lego blocks
Magnets
Magnifying glass
Marbles
Markers
Marshmallows,
  large
Marshmallows,
  mini
Measuring cups
Measuring spoons
Mint, dried

Mint, fresh
Mittens
Napkins
Newspaper,
  shredded
Newspaper, whole
Note cards
Oatmeal, cooked
Oatmeal, dry
Olive oil
Onion powder
Paint, acrylic
Paint, finger
Paint, latex
Paint, tempera
Paint stirring
  sticks
Paintbrush
Paper bags, large
Paper bags, small
Paper punch
Paper towels
Pencils
Pens
Pepper
Pinecones
Pipe cleaners
Plastic animals
Playdough
Pliers
Plungers
Pots and pans
Potting soil
Pulley
Rain
Rice, cooked
Rice, raw

Rope
Rubber bands
Ruler
Sand
Sawdust
Scissors
Shaving cream
Shells
Shoes
Snow
Socks
Sponges
Spoons
Spray bottle
Stapler
Sticks, large
Sticks, medium
Sticks, small
Sticky notes
Stones, medium

Stones, small

Stones. large

Straws, drinking

String

Tape, cellophane

Tape, duct

Tape, electrical

Tape, masking

Tape, painter's

Tape measure

Thread

Tissue paper

Toilet paper

Toothpicks

Tweezers

Vegetable oil

Vegetable shortening

Vinegar

Water, cold

Water, room temperature

Water, warm

Wind, fan-made

Wind, natural

Window screen

Wire

Wood chips

Wooden blocks

Yarn

_____

_____

_____

_____

_____

_____

_____

COMMON PLACES

Cardboard box

Cookie sheet

Floor

In the grass

Inside

Lawn

Outside

Picnic table

Plastic tote

Sandbox

Sidewalk

Sink

Slide

Tabletop

Tub

Under the table

Wading pool

Water

_____

_____

_____

_____

SIMPLE ACTIONS

Beat	Rip
Color	Rub
Count	Scoop
Cut	Scrape
Draw	Share
Glue	Smell
Grab	Sort
Listen	Spill
Look	Stir
Measure	Take turns
Mix	Tape
Paint	Taste
Pinch	Tilt
Pour	Touch

To enhance your experiences experimenting with these lists, we're going to leave you with some tips based on our own experiences with them:

- **Remember that stepping back does not mean leaving.** You need to be on hand to ensure that the children's health and safety are supported, as well as their play.

- **Cover up.** Have old adult-sized shirts for the children to wear to cover their own clothing completely, or make sure you have spare clothes for them to change into.

- **Control the environment.** For example, remove items you don't want to get messy and keep soap and water handy for cleanup.

- **Be considerate.** Have wooden spoons available for those children who want to play but would rather not stick their hands into whatever the concoction happens to be.

- **Give yourself and the children plenty of time.** These are not "Hurry up!" activities.

- **Relax.** The mess probably looks bigger than it is, and most of it will wash up. Remember that kids are empathetic little critters, and your stress affects their play, focus, and mood.

- **Skip it.** If you're having an off day and feeling stressed or unfocused, then do something that's easy and natural for you, even if it doesn't fit into your new play philosophy. The children can sense your stress and won't fully enjoy the experience anyway.

- **Have plenty for everyone.** Having plenty of things on hand is vital. Nothing is worse than realizing you don't have enough of whatever the item is for that last group of children, especially if you promised everyone a turn.

- **Play in shifts.** If you have nine children in your care, you don't have to have all nine children covered in shaving cream. Find out who really wants to go first, and then draw names, fair and square. Remind the children that everyone who wants a turn will get one. (This also helps develop social skills: sometimes in life, you have to wait your turn.)

- **Document.** Make sure you take a few pictures, shoot a few minutes of video, or jot down some notes so you can share your experience with others and document learning. We know caregivers who post pictures to video soon after the activity ends so parents can check in from work on the day's happenings. Documentation helps parents see that play really is learning.

- **Have fun.** Enjoy, see, and share all the learning that is occurring!

We hope you pick items from the three lists, drop this book, and run off to play right now—but take baby steps. If you try to change too much too fast, you're likely to get overwhelmed and run back to the safety and structure of your planning. Evolving from a rigid planner into an (un)curriculum ninja will take time and effort, but the tips from Denita's journey and the three lists of play ideas intended to help you shake things up will help. Once you see the pride a child experiences when she leads, you'll be hooked.

After you play a bit, we hope you come back for the next chapter about evaluating learning. Caregivers cannot make play a powerful force in the lives of children unless they successfully show others how effective it is in building brains and preparing young children for later academic learning. So go play, but hurry back.

Tests, Evaluations, and Assessments . . . Oh My!

In stark contrast to their peers in many other countries, Finnish children do not enter formal school until the calendar year in which they turn seven. Their early childhood is spent at home or in nurseries where play is king. When they finally do reach school, they enjoy short days, long vacations, and plenty of music, art, and sports. Finland also keeps competition to a minimum. It tracks the performance of individual schools but does not publish the findings. Unless parents ask for it, students are not graded until they are thirteen years old; instead they get written report cards from their teachers and do a lot of Reggio-style self-evaluation from an early age.

> —Carl Honoré, *Under Pressure: How The Epidemic of Hyper-Parenting Is Endangering Childhood*

The issue isn't which test is used, or what the test tests. The problem is that young kids' brains just aren't done yet.

> —Po Bronson and Ashley Merryman, *NurtureShock: New Thinking about Children*

If you've made it to this final chapter, then it's going to come as no surprise to you that we have an (un)approach to testing, evaluation, and assessments. Young children's brains aren't done developing, and it's hard to assess or evaluate something that's incomplete. Da Vinci's *Mona Lisa*, Hendrix's cover of "All Along the Watchtower," and Wright's Fallingwater would hardly have been judged masterpieces if they'd been evaluated before they were complete. The best that assessment, testing, and evaluation can do with the minds of young children is capture a moment in time. Check out chapter 5 of *NurtureShock*, "The Search for Intelligent Life in Kindergarten," for more on this topic.

It's reasonable for concerned adults to want to know how children are progressing developmentally, but they need to be thoughtful about what's being assessed, how it's assessed, and what's done with the information collected. Taken to extremes, assessment stresses caregivers, worries parents, and frustrates children. "Overfocus on measurements, performance, evaluations, and other control systems inadvertently breeds stories of blame," writes Annette Simmons (2006, 2297) in *The Story Factor: Inspiration, Influence, and Persuasion Through the Art of Storytelling*. "As flawed human beings we understandably avoid constant surveillance. Despite good intentions, constant monitoring breeds anxiety." When almost-four-year-old Olaf is assessed and everyone in his life learns that he can identify only three letters, Mommy and Daddy start thinking about sending him to a more rigorous academic preschool. Grandma clicks her tongue in disappointment. The neighbors, whose daughter is the same age and who knows all her letters, offer support and revel in the superiority of their child.

Most assessment methods are not reliable determinants of a young child's present knowledge or future performance, and they devalue the individual. Caregivers and teachers working directly with children understand this, but the farther away you get from the classroom, the less people understand this. "Support for testing seems to grow as you move away from the students, going from teacher to principal to central office administrator to school board member to state board member, state legislator, and governor," writes Alfie Kohn in his superb article "Fighting the Tests: A Practical Guide to Rescuing Our Schools" (2001, 350). Testing is great—as long as people other than children are taking the tests. We doubt that any school board, state legislature, teachers union, or other group of adults in this nation will enact standardized testing to determine their own competency levels anytime soon. Mandated testing is a way for policy makers to look as if they're addressing educational issues. Testing is also a smoke screen that allows policy makers to shift the blame to things like "bad schools" or "incompetent teachers."

We talked to a kindergarten teacher who spends about two weeks of each quarter doing the one-on-one evaluations with students required by her district. The intent of these evaluations is to help her gauge progress, see gaps in knowledge, plan future lessons, and understand her students' abilities, but she says she knows these things before the evaluations occur because she knows her students. She dedicates herself to creating strong emotional environments and is a keen observer. She says she knows the formal evaluation process is inadequate compared to real-world observation because it's forced and unnatural. The children feel nervous, and she is rushed. In the end, she says, she goes through the motions and does all the paperwork and files the evaluations as she's supposed to, but she never discovers anything she didn't already know. "It's a waste of eight weeks every year that we could have devoted to rich, hands-on play. We could have created experiences that would have filled in the gaps for some kids and helped others solidify their knowledge." The instructional video that came with the assessment tool she uses suggests the teacher find a quiet spot in the room for the one-on-one evaluations and to do them while the rest of the class is engaged in an activity. While the assessment process looked simple and straightforward in the video, the on-the-ground reality of doing it in a class of twenty-four kindergartners was not idyllic.

Formal evaluation and assessment can be full of pressure, stress, boredom, and confusion—for kids and adults. The kids are typically tossed into the evaluation scenario unaware of what's about to take place or anxious after weeks of unofficial preparation. Either way, many are nervous, anxious, confused, overwhelmed, or bored. Some kids become physically ill from the pressure testing creates for them because the experience falls so far outside their comfort zones. Because he was so anxious, Jeff once blew chunks during a test in early elementary school—and then was accused by his teacher of faking the anxiety as he wiped partially digested SpaghettiOs off his shirt collar and watched the custodian sweep up a mix of his lunch and sawdust.

Adults giving the assessments have the same reactions—they just vomit less. Some feel uncomfortable because the assessment process is far removed from their normal day; it's outside their comfort zone. Others say assessment isn't what they signed up for. One center-based provider said, "I started working here to support children's learning, to play, not to do these mind-draining assessments." Many adults are overwhelmed (or underwhelmed) by the assessment tool itself. Another caregiver, describing an assessment tool that's used nationally, told us, "This thing seems like it was written by a team of well-intentioned accountants who had never met a child, not early educators with real-life experience." Some caregivers even feel forced to devote time to teaching to the test, although they themselves would not call it that. Last, there are the cheaters. Some teachers feel so much pressure that they've gone so far as to fix answers on tests. *Freakonomics: A Rogue Economist Explores the Hidden Side of Everything* by Steven D. Levitt and Stephen J. Dubner details this kind of teacher cheating in Chicago.

Think this doesn't happen in preschool programs? As academics creep deeper and deeper into early childhood programs, cheating is becoming more and more prevalent in programs serving preschoolers. Sometimes it happens because parents are driven to ensure that their perfect baby gets into the right program. Other times, programs fudge the numbers to guarantee funding and other community support.

Like the kindergarten teacher mentioned above, many caregivers we talked to pay little or no attention to the findings of the evaluations and assessments they're required to complete. At this end of the spectrum assessments are filed away, and the work of knowing children through strong emotional environments and supporting learning through engaging physical environments continues.

In the middle of the evaluation and assessment spectrum, there are those who fuss and fiddle with the results as they calculate mean averages and standard deviations to tease out meaning and see causes and connections. These thoughtful statisticians seek to find valuable trends and insights hidden in the raw numbers to develop a clearer big picture of the state of learning at a moment in time.

At the other end of this spectrum, some people believe childhood would be much more organized and orderly if the heuristic early learning process were wholly quantified and broken down into a series of elegant and dependable algorithms. Unfortunately, pushing so hard for achievements on tests and evaluations can kill off the desire to learn and try new things. Carl Honoré writes in *Under Pressure: How the Epidemic of*

Hyper-Parenting Is Endangering Childhood, "Scores of studies have shown that the more people are encouraged to chase results and rewards—an A+ on the report card, say—the less interest they take in the task itself" (2008, 121).

At one end, the results of assessments are not valued, while at the other, assessments are overvalued; in the middle, where thoughtful work is being attempted, the results are often meaningless because of the flawed tools, faulty methods, and cheating we mentioned earlier.

One experienced caregiver told us that her biggest worry about the future of her profession is "societal pressure to teach and test children in developmentally inappropriate ways." Another writes, "I am increasingly concerned that we are harming our children with all of the academic and testing demands that we place on them at such a young age. I understand the need for accountability, but there are better ways to obtain the information necessary. It should not be at the expense of the children."

Remember Denita's story in chapter 6 about her conversation with Avery's dad, Brian? Little Avery spent her preschool years in a program in which rhyming was part of daily life, and rhymes did not necessarily have to be words—*calloon*, *falloon*, *spalloon* were all accepted as perfectly good rhymes for *balloon*. As far as Denita and Brian know, the first time Avery heard the word *titties* was when it came out of her own mouth as she searched for a rhyme for *kitties*. Yet although she was an experienced and creative rhyme finder, the stress, strangeness, and structure of the kindergarten assessment failed to pick it up. Some preschool programs have even turned to practicing for kindergarten assessments in an attempt to avoid this kind of error, which turns the programs into what the organization FairTest (www.fairtest.org) would call a test prep center.

Don't Feed the Beast

When it comes to tests, evaluations, and assessments, our general advice is this: don't feed the beast. Don't give in to the push to devote so much time and energy and so many resources to standardized tests, evaluations, and assessments that push early academics and devour childhood. "We must make the fight against standardized tests our top priority because, until we have chased this monster from the schools, it will be difficult, perhaps even impossible, to pursue the kinds of reforms that can truly improve teaching and learning," writes Alfie Kohn (2001, 351). The same can be said of preschool assessments and evaluations; they are all teeth of the same beast. Freeing the children in your care from the jaws of the beast and giving back their playtime is necessary if you want to chase testing from your program. You can do it. Denita did.

From Denita's World

I used to evaluate in order to be a more "official" preschool. I had what I called a Look What I Can Do book for every child, in which I celebrated what each one knew. These books contained copies of simple assessments I completed regularly to determine where the kids were developmentally. The idea of the books—to document learning—was fine, but the way I went about finding out what the children knew was horrible. I would periodically take one child at a time and sit with her, pointing to letters and so forth, trying to figure out what she knew. It was awful—the other kids were playing, and the child I had corralled wanted to play too. It was extremely fake, and I hated it as much as the kids did, but I felt I had to do it in order to keep my families.

Then I just stopped doing it—without a warning or a letter or any notice. It has been years now since I stopped, and I've had only one family ask to see their child's book. Holding my breath, I explained that I wasn't doing formal assessments anymore. I told them I was trusting the kids as learners and trusting my own observational skills as a caregiver and educator. To my complete relief, the dad, who is also an educator, said, "That's good. That's the way they want us to teach."

If caregivers, teachers, directors, and administrators refuse to feed the testing, evaluation, and assessment beast, it will shrink and have less control of our time, energy, and resources—and this will free those up for thoughtful, experience-based learning.

Assess and Evaluate This

While we do urge you to push back the assessment beast, we do believe there are three things that should be assessed and evaluated to help assure safe and healthy play and learning. Those three things are:

- **Vision.** Kids who have problems seeing have a hard time—our world is such a visual place. A blurry and unclear view of it can affect everything from walking to reading. Regular vision tests will pick up abnormalities so corrections can be made. The earlier vision problems are caught, the better.

- **Hearing.** Like vision, hearing is a conduit to a great deal of information, and hearing problems can influence everything from balance to speech. Hearing evaluations can catch problems and lead to useful tools. Catching a hearing issue at age three instead of in third grade, for instance, can have a huge impact on a child's learning.

- **Things that make you go hmm.** We also think you should note and look into any persistent anomalies you detect during your day-to-day observation of a child. Awareness of things that set your Spidey Sense to tingling, combined with thoughtful action, can lead to early detection and intervention. Sometimes you observe weird actions and behaviors in children because they are on curious journeys to know the world and try out different ways of being. Other times, you observe weird actions and behaviors in children because something is up. In addition, sudden changes in a child's demeanor, unusual eye-contact patterns, or delays in developmental milestones can signal potential situations like abuse, autism, or physiological problems. Be aware. Trust your gut. Take action when you need to.

Trust Children's Self-Assessment and Self-Evaluation

Adults need to know how kids are doing, but when it comes to evaluating, testing, and assessing physical, cognitive, and social development, step back and trust the children to do so themselves—or more accurately, step back and trust that they're already doing it. To know how the children are doing, more than anything else, we just need to pay attention. From their earliest days, children instinctively evaluate and assess their knowledge and ability to step out of their safety zones to try something new. They constantly test their own abilities and knowledge—and their limits. They are always calculating what they know and what they need to know—and how to go about knowing it. Most infants go through stages in which they drop spoons, toy keys, and binkies and then wait to see what happens: Does it float to the ceiling? Does it fall to the floor? Does it get picked up and given back? Does it get picked up and put out of reach? Does it just sit there? At some point, though, this game/experiment stops. Why? Because the child has learned what she can from it and is ready to move on to a new experiment—though she may come back and retest now and again to make sure gravity still works and that Mommy will give her back the keys. Children take their first steps because they have self-assessed their abilities and know that they are ready. They write a *B* instead of a scribble because they have determined they are ready for *B*s. They speak new words to others for the first time after practicing and testing their skills in the privacy of their own cribs.

The failure of adults to see the extent of children's consistent, high-quality, useful self-evaluation and self-assessment doesn't mean it isn't there. It just means adults need to look closer and pay better attention. Jeff remembers when his son Tyler was about two years old and busy on a playground structure. After lots of climbing and sliding, Tyler stood on the very edge of a platform and reached for the pole he'd seen the older children sliding down. Jeff's inclination was to rush over to stop or catch Tyler, but Tyler's eyes glimmered with confidence and calm as he stepped into thin air and slid down the pole. Tyler had evaluated and assessed his abilities and knew that he was ready to try, that he was up to the attempt. His busy little brain calculated that his large muscles, depth perception, self-confidence, coordination, kinesthetic awareness, and problem-solving skills were up to the challenge at hand—and they were. He assessed the situation better than his daddy. Children do this kind of thing all the time; adults are just not usually tuned-in enough to notice.

The self-assessment of children needs to be supported. Adults should help children build on their own evaluations. Activities like conversation, open-ended questions, and simply trusting in the power of play offer children this type of support. Here are several ways you can support children's self-assessment:

- **Hold microconversations throughout the course of the day.** To offer ongoing support, engage children in short, casual conversations about what they're doing, why they're doing it, what went right and what went wrong, how they plan to proceed with a project, and how they could have proceeded differently in the past. All of these sorts of conversations help children expand their skills, build self-understanding, and think about how they think. Thinking about how you think is called *metacognition*, and it's crucial to later academic success.

- **Ask open-ended questions.** Ask questions like "How's that working out for you, Ginger?" or "Hey, Professor, what happened when you mixed the liquid soap with the fingerpaint?" Help children pause and evaluate their actions. Again, you can do this throughout the course of the day without obstructing the flow of an activity.

- **Trust play.** Understand that children are constantly assessing their abilities and skills while they play. In fact, they're also testing and expanding their abilities and skills. Your willingness to step back a bit and trust their process is hugely supportive.

In the end, the goals of supporting self-assessment are to unobtrusively help children develop self-awareness and metacognition. Adults need to be unobtrusive so the flow of play is not interrupted and they don't steal any of the power and control children have while they play. Being self-aware and being able to think about their thinking are tools children can depend on their whole lives. These tools help children and adults make thoughtful choices about situations based on past experiences.

Child: Last time I pulled the cat's tail, I got scratched. I'm not going to do that again.

Adult: Last time I drove this stretch of road, I got a speeding ticket. Better slow down.

These tools also help evaluate actions.

Child: Was it a good idea to ride my bike off the garage roof?

Adult: Maybe I should have called an electrician.

Document

Tracking learning should be a joyful practice that documents a child's journey as a learner. Unfortunately, through formalized assessments, tests, and evaluations, we've turned it into a chore, one more focused on process and ritual than on actual learning. We've set arbitrary time limits, scripted the process, and even standardized the writing utensils and the shapes we fill in with them. Where, oh where, would society be without number 2 pencils and those little ovals to fill in?

Be a documentor, not an assessor or evaluator. Your job should be that of archivist, historian, or reporter. You should be more interested in documenting the process of early learning than in handing out stars, stickers, smiley faces, letter grades, or canned comments like "Great Job" scribbled in red pencil. You should document what children have learned and use that information to support children's learning journey, not to figure out what to try to teach them next, based on an arbitrary curriculum.

These days Denita explains to the parents in her program that she can see the children's learning in their play and that she uses what she observes them learning now to support their future learning. If she sees something that raises her concern—something that starts her Spidey Sense to tingling—then she can take action, because she trusts her abilities as a quiet observer. She also uses conversations, e-mail, text messages, notes, and photos to give parents examples of what their child is doing during the day, and she describing what the kids are learning while they're playing. Denita and the kids have conversations and document their play and learning in memory books, which are basically albums of pictures with explanatory captions. Parents can then look through these books and gain a lot of understanding about their child's learning.

A tower of blocks, a painting, or a collage made with Popsicle sticks, feathers, and cotton balls may be a neat creation, but the process the child used to make it is usually more significant. The documentation you should collect should not be limited to finished products, because in most cases you can learn more about the children from their processes. Pay close attention to the same basic questions reporters are trained to investigate: Who, What, Where, When, Why, and How. Keep these questions in mind as you observe children at work. When you do, you'll be on your way to seeing their processes clearly.

Process is important in documentation too. Here are some tools you should consider using:

- **Portfolios.** Brought home one at a time and hung on the refrigerator, children's projects can become clutter, but collections of their creations over time can offer real insight into their developmental path, temperament, ways of learning and knowing the world, interests, and personalities. Look back at a child's art projects from age one to age five, and you will see his progression from scribbler to writer and from experiencer to thinker. You can store these documents in many ways, ranging from a simple cardboard folder to a scanned electronic version on a zip drive. Children should also have the chance to help select what goes in their portfolio. For example, consider asking them to pick out their best work, things they are especially proud of, or those they put lots of effort into. This gives them ownership of the process and empowers them to self-evaluate.

- **Photographs.** Pictures are worth more than a thousand words and are useful tools in documenting the course a child sets for his learning. When documenting with photos, you should focus on catching real-life action shots of kids fully engaged in a moment rather than staged and posed shots. Pictures can be printed or stored electronically. Add them to portfolios or create individual memory books. We've also heard from many caregivers who are using e-mail and social media like Facebook to share play-based learning in close to real time with parents.

- **Video and audio recordings.** Recorders are so inexpensive and easy to use that there is no reason why caregivers should not be documenting play and learning with them. Most devices require little more than pointing and clicking to capture moments. As with photographs, the best moments to catch are the real-life, not the posed, ones. These items are also easy to share with parents and save for posterity. One caution we have is that capturing learning moments should not get in the way of the moment itself. The mere presence of the device can alter the moment for many children. Our advice is to be mindful and unobtrusive—and know that not every second of a child's life needs to be recorded.

- **Conversations.** Old-fashioned but reliable, simple conversation is a good way to document learning, because you can use leading conversation and open-ended questions to probe a child's thinking process. Talk to children a lot and jot down simple notes about what you discuss. These notes can be added to their portfolios or recorded electronically for your own reference.

Do Something with Documentation

Documentation of early learning is only valuable if you actually do something with what you have learned. Years ago, during Jeff's days as a child care and community center director, staff he worked with documented observations during a six-year-old's summer camp experience. They documented little things, like repeatedly missing the cue ball while playing bumper pool; frustration while reading, writing, and drawing; headaches after reading, writing and drawing; and subpar dodge ball skills. The child's parents took him to have his vision tested after reviewing the incidents documented by the staff, and the little guy showed up a few days later with a pair of glasses. That first pair got broken a few hours later during a game of Crazy Basketball when he caught a ball with his face, but after a few weeks of wearing the replacement pair, his bumper pool, reading, writing, drawing, and dodge ball skills improved, the headaches went away, and the following school year was much more successful. The point is that documentation is useless when it just sits in a filing cabinet or on a flash drive. Here's a quick overview of ways in which thoughtful documentation of the processes of early learning can be useful:

- **Documentation can chart next steps.** Documentation provides a road map of where a child has been and where a child is going as a learner, and it is useful in preparing for future learning—seeing current abilities will help you understand how to build new experiences to expand knowledge.

- **Reviewing documentation can help caregivers see things about a child that they may have missed before.** Caregivers may be able to see, for instance, a growing interest in butterflies or a deterioration in small-muscle skills. Reviewing documentation offers deeper insight into children's thinking and clearer understanding about what is going on in their lives.

- **Documentation helps parents, funders, regulators, and others see the learning that is happening—and *how* it is happening.** This can lead to greater buy-in from these groups as well as appreciation and understanding.

  - Documentation is a valuable tool for refining process, honing strategies, and thinking about the big picture.

  - Documentation helps caregivers see holes in a child's knowledge or delays in development that are not otherwise obvious.

  - Documentation shows children that their efforts are valuable and meaningful.

We suggest you document for all these reasons and share the results with children, parents, supporters, funders, regulators, and any others who could benefit. Our experience tells us that people are more responsive to these real, three-dimensional examples of learning than they are to flat columns of numbers or pie charts. Documentation of a child's progress with the methods we've described shares a story about learning moments. Sharing it provides richer insight and deeper understanding than a regimented assessment could. When you share your documentation, explain why the learning moments you have included are important: What was that child learning with the paint-covered flyswatter? How long did the girls in that video play in the refrigerator box, and how did doing so build social skills? What does playing with scissors and glue have to do with learning to read?

Another thing we suggest you do with your documentation is evaluate yourself and your program. Use it to take a good look at how well you are nurturing children as individuals, building engaging experiences, trusting children, slowing the rush of childhood, pushing back against the push for early academics, and utilizing your physical space. Does your documentation show lots of variety that feeds the different ways children know the world? Have you cut out screen time? Have you let children lead? Have you valued play?

Your documentation should provide a clear picture of the quality of the play and learning in your program. It can also serve as a road map for future changes.

Some books on documentation you might want to read are:

Margie Carter and Deb Curtis's books *The Art of Awareness, Designs for Living and Learning*, and *Learning Together with Young Children*

Susan Stacey's books *The Unscripted Classroom* and *Emergent Curriculum in Early Childhood Settings*

Assessment is an important part of early learning, but it does not have to painfully suck the fun out of play or cause so much stress in teachers and kids. In fact, it can be a fun process if you enact some of the suggestions in this chapter. Remember: take baby steps—too much change too quickly can lead to chaos.

Now, for the hard part. In a few sentences, you'll be done reading this book and you'll have to make a decision—what are you going to do next?

Option 1: You can set the book down and continue to do things the way you've always done them. This book, and all the ideas we've shared in it, will end up forgotten on a shelf or stuck in a pile on your office floor or tossed in a box in the closet.

Option 2: You can make a change. You can take a few baby steps toward a child-led, (un)planned (un)curriculum. You can give up some control and trust kids as learners. You can tweak your emotional and physical environments to better support play. You can advocate for play and for childhood. You can dig your Barbies and your Tonka trucks out of that box in the basement and remember the way play used to be. You can simply let them play.

We hope you choose option 2. If you do, and you decide you need more support or want to connect with other people who have made this same choice, come find us at www.facebook.com/LetThemPlayBook. We'd love to help support your efforts to build an (un)curriculum, hear your success stories, and find ways to work together to value play and defend childhood.

Thanks for reading. Now go play.

References

Bardige, Betty Lynn Segal. 2005. *At a Loss for Words: How America Is Failing Our Children and What We Can Do about It*. Philadelphia: Temple University Press.

Brown, Stuart, with Christopher Vaughan. 2009. *Play: How It Shapes the Brain, Opens the Imagination, and Invigorates the Soul*. New York: Avery.

Bruer, John T. 1999. *The Myth of the First Three Years: A New Understanding of Early Brain Development and Lifelong Learning*. New York: Free Press.

Carlsson-Paige, Nancy. 2008. *Taking Back Childhood: A Proven Roadmap for Raising Confident, Creative, Compassionate Kids*. New York: Plume.

Challenge Success. 2011. "Facts on How Narrow Definitions of Success Adversely Affect Our Children." http://challengesuccess.org/ Portals/29/Docs/Challenge-Success-Do-You-Know.pdf.

Copeland, Kristen A., Susan N. Sherman, Cassandra A. Kendeigh, Heidi J. Kalkwarf, and Brian E. Saelens. 2012. "Societal Values and Policies May Curtail Preschool Children's Physical Activity in Child Care Centers." *Pediatrics* 129 (2): 1–10. http://pediatrics.aappublications.org/content/early/2012/01/02/peds.2011-2012.full.pdf.

Darling-Kuria, Nikki. 2010. *Brain-Based Early Learning Activities: Connecting Theory and Practice*. St. Paul, MN: Redleaf.

Elkind, David. 2007. *The Hurried Child: Growing Up Too Fast Too Soon*. Reading, MA: Addison-Wesley.

Gladwell, Malcolm. 2000. *The Tipping Point: How Little Things Can Make a Big Difference*. New York: Little, Brown.

Godin, Seth. 2010. *Linchpin: Are You Indispensable?* New York: Portfolio.

———. 2010. "Whatever Happened to Labor?" *Seth Godin's Blog*. http://sethgodin.typepad.com/seths_blog/2010/09/whatever-happened-to-labor.html.

Hirsh-Pasek, Kathy, and Roberta Michnick Golinkoff. 2003. *Einstein Never Used Flash Cards: How Our Children Really Learn—and Why They Need to Play More and Memorize Less*. Emmaus, PA: Rodale.

Honoré, Carl. 2008. *Under Pressure: How The Epidemic of Hyper-Parenting Is Endangering Childhood*. Toronto: Knopf Canada.

Kohn, Alfie. 2001. "Fighting the Tests: A Practical Guide to Rescuing Our Schools." *Phi Delta Kappan* 82 (5): 349–57. www.alfiekohn.org/teaching/ftt.htm.

Levitt, Steven D., and Stephen J. Dubner. 2009. *Freakonomics: A Rogue Economist Explores the Hidden Side of Everything.* New York: Harper Perennial.

Lips, Dan, Shanea Watkins, and John Fleming. 2008. *Does Spending More on Education Improve Academic Achievement?* The Heritage Foundation. http://www.heritage.org/research/reports/2008/09/does-spending-more-on-education-improve-academic-achievement.

Louv, Richard. 2008. *Last Child in the Woods: Saving Our Children from Nature-Deficit Disorder.* Rev. ed. Chapel Hill, NC: Algonquin.

Marano, Hara Estroff. 2008. *A Nation of Wimps: The High Cost of Invasive Parenting.* New York: Broadway.

Medina, John. 2008. *Brain Rules: 12 Principles for Surviving and Thriving at Work, Home, and School.* Seattle: Pear.

Milteer, Regina M., and Kenneth R. Ginsburg. 2011. "The Importance of Play in Promoting Healthy Child Development and Maintaining Strong Parent-Child Bond: Focus on Children in Poverty." *Pediatrics* 129 (1): e204–e213. http://pediatrics.aappublications.org/content/early/2011/12/21/peds.2011-2953.full.pdf.

Mintz, Steven. 2004. *Huck's Raft: A History of American Childhood.* Cambridge, MA: Belknap Press of Harvard University.

National Scientific Council on the Developing Child. 2007. *The Timing and Quality of Early Experiences Combine to Shape Brain Architecture: Working Paper #5.* Harvard University. http://developingchild.harvard.edu/index.php/download_file/-/view/74/.

———. 2009. *Drive: The Surprising Truth about What Motivates Us.* New York: Riverhead.

Puckett, Margaret B., and Janet K. Black. 2007. *Understanding Infant Development.* St. Paul, MN: Redleaf.

———. 2007. *Understanding Toddler Development.* St. Paul, MN: Redleaf.

Simmons, Annette. 2006. *The Story Factor: Inspiration, Influence, and Persuasion Through the Art of Storytelling.* New York: Basic.

Stearns, Peter N. 2006. *Childhood in World History.* New York: Routledge.

Thomas, Susan Gregory. 2007. *Buy, Buy Baby: How Consumer Culture Manipulates Parents and Harms Young Minds.* Boston: Houghton Mifflin.

US Department of Education. 2009. "Race to the Top Fact Sheet." www2.ed.gov/programs/racetothetop/factsheet.html.

Suggested Reading

Are We Scaring Ourselves to Death? How Pessimism, Paranoia, and a Misguided Media Are Leading Us toward Disaster by H. Aaron Cohl

The Art of Awareness: How Observation Can Transform Your Teaching by Deb Curtis and Margie Carter

Arts with the Brain in Mind by Eric Jensen

At a Loss for Words: How America Is Failing Our Children and What We Can Do about It by Betty Bardige

Babies in the Rain by Jeff A. Johnson

Beyond Behavior Management: The Six Life Skills Children Need to Thrive in Today's World by Jenna Bilmes

Blind Spots: Why Smart People Do Dumb Things by Madeleine L. Van Hecke

Born to Buy: The Commercialized Child and the New Consumer Culture by Juliet B. Schor

Brain-Based Early Learning Activities: Connecting Theory and Practice by Nikki Darling-Kuria

Brain-Based Learning: The New Paradigm of Teaching by Eric P. Jensen

Brain Rules: 12 Principles for Surviving and Thriving at Work, Home, and School by John Medina

The Brain That Changes Itself: Stories of Personal Triumph from the Frontiers of Brain Science by Norman Doidge

Buy, Buy Baby by Susan Gregory Thomas

The Case for Mixed-Age Grouping in Early Education by Lilian G. Katz, Demetra Evangelou, and Jeanette Allison Hartman

Childhood in World History by Peter N. Stearns

Consuming Kids: The Hostile Takeover of Childhood by Susan Linn

Creative Experiences for Young Children, 3rd edition, by Mimi Brodsky Chenfeld

Creativity: Flow and Psychology of Discovery and Invention by Mihaly Csikszentmihalyi

Dear Parent: Caring for Infants with Respect, 2nd edition, by Magda Gerber and Joan Weaver

Democracy and Education by John Dewey

Do-It-Yourself Early Learning by Jeff A. Johnson and Tasha A. Johnson

Drive: The Surprising Truth about What Motivates Us by Daniel H. Pink

Einstein Never Used Flash Cards: How Our Children Really Learn—and Why They Need to Play More and Memorize Less by Kathy Hirsh-Pasek and Roberta Michnick Golinkoff

The Element: How Finding Your Passion Changes Everything by Ken Robinson

Emergent Curriculum in Early Childhood Settings by Susan Stacey

Emergent Literacy and Dramatic Play in Early Education by Jane Davidson

Even More Fizzle, Bubble, Pop & WOW! by Lisa Murphy

Everyday Early Learning by Jeff A. Johnson and Zoë Johnson

The Evolving Self: A Psychology for the Third Millennium by Mihaly Csikszentmihalyi

Finding Flow: The Psychology of Engagement with Everyday Life by Mihaly Csikszentmihalyi

Finding Your Smile Again: A Child Care Professional's Guide to Reducing Stress and Avoiding Burnout by Jeff A. Johnson

Five Minds for the Future by Howard Gardner

Flow: The Psychology of Optimal Experience by Mihaly Csikszentmihalyi

Fostering Children's Social Competence: The Teacher's Role by Lilian G. Katz and Diane E. McCellan

Free-Range Kids: Giving Our Children the Freedom We Had without Going Nuts with Worry by Lenore Skenazy

How Children Fail by John Holt

How Children Learn by John Holt

How Children Play by Ingeborg Haller

Huck's Raft: A History of American Childhood by Steven Mintz

The Hurried Child: Growing Up Too Fast Too Soon by David Elkind

Infant/Toddler Caregiving: A Guide to Setting Up Environments by J. Ronald Lally and Jay Stewart

Infant/Toddler Caregiving: A Guide to Social-Emotional Growth and Socialization by California Department of Education, edited by J. Ronald Lally

Keeping Your Smile: Caring for Children with Joy, Love, and Intention by Jeff A. Johnson

Keys to Solution in Brief Therapy by Steve de Shazer

Last Child in the Woods: Saving Our Children from Nature-Deficit Disorder by Richard Louv

Learning All the Time by John Holt

Linchpin: Are You Indispensable? by Seth Godin

Miseducation: Preschoolers at Risk by David Elkind

The Montessori Method by Maria Montessori

More Than Miracles: The State of the Art of Solution-Focused Brief Therapy
    by Steve de Shazer and Yvonne Dolan

The Myth of the First Three Years: A New Understanding of Early Brain Develop-
    ment and Lifelong Learning by John T. Bruer

A Nation of Wimps: The High Cost of Invasive Parenting by Hara Estroff Marano

NurtureShock: New Thinking about Children by Po Bronson
    and Ashley Merryman

The Ooey Gooey Handbook by Lisa Murphy

Out of our Minds: Learning to be Creative by Ken Robinson

Parent Power! by John Rosemond

Play = Learning: How Play Motivates and Enhances Children's Cognitive and
    Social-Emotional Growth, edited by Dorothy G. Singer, Roberta Michnick
    Golinkoff, and Kathy Hirsh-Pasek

Play—the Foundation That Supports the House of Higher Learning
    by Lisa Murphy

Play: How It Shapes the Brain, Opens the Imagination, and Invigorates the Soul
    by Stuart Brown with Christopher Vaughan

Play: The Pathway from Theory to Practice by Sandra Heidemann and
    Deborah Hewitt

Playing to Get Smart by Elizabeth Jones and Renatta M. Cooper

The Power of Play: Learning What Comes Naturally by David Elkind

The Quality School Teacher by William Glasser

Ready or Not: Leadership Choices in Early Care and Education by Stacie G. Goffin
    and Valora Washington

Right from Birth: Building Your Child's Foundation for Life: Birth to 18 Months
    by Craig T. Ramey and Sharon L. Ramey

Secure Relationships by Alice Sterling Honig

Seeking Balance in an Unbalanced World: A Teacher's Journey
    by Angela Schmidt Fishbaugh

So Sexy So Soon: The New Sexualized Childhood, and What Parents Can Do to
    Protect Their Kids by Diane E. Levin and Jean Kilbourne

Social and Emotional Development: Connecting Science and Practice in Early Childhood Settings by Dave Riley, Robert R. San Juan, Joan Klinkner, and Ann Ramminger

Taking Back Childhood: A Proven Roadmap for Raising Confident, Creative, Compassionate Kids by Nancy Carlsson-Paige

Teaching by Heart by Mimi Brodsky Chenfeld

Teaching the 3 Cs: Creativity, Curiosity, and Courtesy by Patricia Dischler

Teaching with the Brain in Mind by Eric P. Jensen

The Ten Faces of Innovation: IDEO's Strategies for Beating the Devil's Advocate and Driving Creativity throughout Your Organization by Thomas Kelley

Under Pressure: How the Epidemic of Hyper-Parenting Is Endangering Childhood by Carl Honoré

Understanding Infant Development by Margaret B. Puckett and Janet K. Black

Understanding Temperament by Lyndall Shick

Understanding Toddler Development by Margaret B. Puckett and Janet K. Black

The Unscripted Classroom by Susan Stacey

A Whole New Mind: Moving from the Informational Age to the Conceptual Age by Daniel H. Pink

The Youngest Minds by Ann B. Barnet and Richard J. Barnet

Your Self-Confident Baby: How to Encourage Your Child's Natural Abilities—from the Very Start by Magda Gerber and Allison Johnson

Zen Habits: Handbook for Life by Leo Babauta

Suggested Websites and Blogs

Alfie Kohn—www.alfiekohn.org/articles_subject.htm#null

Alliance for Childhood—www.allianceforchildhood.org

John Medina's Blog—http://brainrules.blogspot.com

Caregivers Unboxed—http://caregiversunboxed.com

Challenge Success—www.challengesuccess.org

Daniel Pink— www.danpink.com

Explorations Early Learning—www.explorationsearlylearning.com

FairTest—www.fairtest.org/how-testing-feeds-schooltoprison-pipeline

Results Only Work Environment—www.gorowe.com

Howard Gardner—www.howardgardner.com

International Play Association (US Affiliate)—www.ipausa.org

Lifeways—www.lifewaysnorthamerica.org

National Institute for Play—www.nifplay.org/about_us.html

Lisa Murphy—www.ooeygooey.com

Play Counts—http://playcounts.com

Self-Determination Theory—www.psych.rochester.edu/SDT

Peter Gray's Blog—www.psychologytoday.com/blog/freedom-learn

Resources for Infant Educarers—www.rie.org

John Rosemond—www.rosemond.com

Seth Godin's Blog—http://sethgodin.typepad.com

Steve Spangler—www.stevespanglerscience.com

WestEd—www.wested.org